High-Quality Early Childhood Programs

D1319480

High-Quality Early Childhood Programs

The What, Why, and How

by Laura J. Colker, EdD, and Derry Koralek

 **Redleaf Press**®
www.redleafpress.org
800-423-8309

Par/teach
J
372.21
Col
Main

Published by Redleaf Press
10 Yorkton Court
St. Paul, MN 55117
www.redleafpress.org

© 2018 by Laura J. Colker and Derry Koralek

All rights reserved. Unless otherwise noted on a specific page, no portion
of this publication may be reproduced or transmitted in any form or by
any means, electronic or mechanical, including photocopying, recording,
or capturing on any information storage and retrieval system, without
permission in writing from the publisher, except by a reviewer, who
may quote brief passages in a critical article or review to be printed in a
magazine or newspaper, or electronically transmitted on radio, television,
or the Internet.

First edition 2018
Cover design by Tom Heffron
Cover photograph by iStock.com/Martinan
Interior design by Louise OFarrell
Typeset in Adobe Minion Pro
Interior photos on page ii by iStock.com/Martinan; pages 4, 18, 56, and
    140 by Julia Luckenbill; page 11 by iStock.com/marcduf; page 96 by
    Karen Phillips; and page 125 by iStock.com/SolStock
Printed in the United States of America

24 23 22 21 20 19 18 17   1 2 3 4 5 6 7 8

Library of Congress Cataloging-in-Publication Data
CIP data has been applied for

Printed on acid-free paper

YOUTH SERVICES
Falmouth Public Library
300 Main Street
Falmouth, MA 02540
508-457-2555

Contents

Foreword

When I began my fifty-year career in early childhood education, I thought my degrees in child development and early childhood education had prepared me well to teach young children. I soon realized that good teaching was much more complex than I had anticipated. It was my great fortune to spend that first year of teaching under the guidance of a knowledgeable, thoughtful, and very experienced teacher. I watched how she related with great respect and caring to each child, how she listened with genuine interest to what each child said and did, and how she inspired the children to become collaborative, active, and eager learners. She took the time to explain the "why" of her practices and gave me an increasing role in the classroom. As an education coordinator for Head Start programs in Mississippi and Washington, DC, I developed the skills to support teachers from supervisors who shared what they knew about forging trusting relationships, challenged me to think through tough situations, provided thoughtful suggestions, and encouraged me to try new approaches. These experiences taught me that the most effective professional development occurs within the context of trusting relationships and through in-classroom support.

The early childhood field has grown enormously in the past decades. We now know so much more about effective teaching practices and the importance of early experiences to children's success as learners. As investments in early childhood programs increase, administrators and teachers are held accountable for meeting quality standards and ensuring that children achieve positive outcomes. They must implement a comprehensive curriculum, use ongoing assessment to inform their decisions, ensure the development and learning of all children, and engage families by establishing reciprocal relationships. At the same time, resources are limited, and the guidance and support teachers receive varies greatly.

Teachers in early childhood programs bring a wide range of experiences and knowledge to their role. Every teacher has areas of strength and areas that need strengthening. A new teacher might need help organizing a dynamic and appropriate environment, creating a clear program structure, or guiding children's behavior in positive ways. A more experienced teacher may benefit from targeted support and suggestions for implementing a study, planning small-group experiences, or preparing for a particularly challenging family conference.

There are many ways to gain the skills and knowledge needed to implement a high-quality program: participating in workshops, attending professional conferences, following a comprehensive curriculum, and using an ongoing assessment system all contribute to professional development and effective teaching. I am convinced that the best way to help a teacher develop new skills and gain knowledge is individualized, in-classroom support from a knowledgeable supervisor or coach who takes the time to build a relationship and who is committed to the teacher's success. *High-Quality Early Childhood Programs: The What, Why, and How* is the resource that makes this possible. In one book, you now have a concise summary of the latest research and standards that define a high-quality early childhood program. In the chapters on each age group, there are two types of charts that enable you to quickly access the information you need on the spot. The first identifies what you should see in all components of a high-quality program, including the physical environment, how teachers interact with children, how families are involved, and the kinds of experiences in which children are engaged. The importance of each indicator is explained in the next column. These explanations are invaluable in giving supervisors a way to help teachers understand the theory behind their practices. The second type of chart identifies warning signs that may indicate when the teacher's practices are not appropriate, identifies what the teacher may be thinking, and suggests ways to respond in a supportive manner. The key to responding in a supportive rather than judgmental way is understanding the beliefs that might explain a teacher's inappropriate practices.

This updated and greatly expanded edition of our earlier work is a gift for supervisors of early childhood programs serving infants, toddlers, and preschool children and their families. I am grateful to my original coauthors, Derry and Laura, for reviving a resource that supports the critical role of early childhood educators who supervise, coach, and provide professional development for teachers.

Diane Trister Dodge
Early Childhood Educator
Founder of Teaching Strategies, LLC

Acknowledgments

This book has a long evolution, going back to 1989 when the US Army Child and Youth Services Division contracted with Creative Associates, International to develop *A Handbook for Army Education Program Specialists*. That publication was written by the authors of this book along with Diane T. Dodge, under the direction of M.-A. Lucas, Chief, Army Child and Youth Services. The US Army was then and continues to be the country's largest employer-sponsored child care program. It also is a leader in quality, as exemplified by its motto "Workforce readiness begins with high-quality child care." Under the direction of M.-A. Lucas, the handbook served as a primary resource for the technical assistance provided by Army curriculum and training specialists for caregivers and teachers at installations worldwide. We are grateful to M.-A. Lucas for her vision and support in creating and implementing the use of that initial handbook to foster common benchmarks for quality programming.

Realizing that this same information would be useful to all programs serving infants, toddlers, and preschoolers, the authors broadened and refocused the guide and added content related to quality school-age programs. In 1993 the National Association for the Education of Young Children (NAEYC) published the revised version as *The What, Why, and How of High-Quality Early Childhood Education: A Guide for On-Site Supervision*. A second edition followed in 1995, with subsequent printings in 1998 and 2002. This new publication was widely used by trainers, supervisors, and program directors and as a text in college courses.

Over the decades, early childhood educators, including the authors, have refined the definition of quality. As the field grew, new knowledge and research made it possible to better pinpoint the skills, techniques, and strategies that support children's development and learning. As such, *High-Quality Early Childhood Programs: The What, Why, and How* is an entirely new book, but the goal of the earlier iterations remains true: to provide supervisors and administrators with the tools that allow them to recognize and encourage high-quality programs.

We are grateful to many people who have gotten us to this point. In particular, we would like to thank the many supervisors and teachers who used the earlier publications that led up to this book. Their hard work and passion for helping children and families ignited our own passion to write this book.

In addition, we especially want to acknowledge Diane T. Dodge, our coauthor on both the original handbook and the NAEYC publication. Each of us has collaborated with and been influenced by Diane throughout our careers. Her spirit and inspiration were with us in the writing of this latest book, for which she wrote the foreword.

Laura J. Colker, EdD
Derry Koralek

 Introduction

Welcome to *High-Quality Early Childhood Programs: The What, Why, and How.* This book is for educators who oversee, supervise, coach, or provide professional development for teachers in early childhood programs serving children from infancy through age five. Whether you are a child development program director or assistant director, elementary school principal or assistant principal, an education or curriculum specialist, an early childhood consultant, or someone interested in promoting high-quality early childhood education, this book should help you in both your day-to-day work and in planning and assessing your program. This volume replaces an earlier version of the book *The What, Why, and How of High-Quality Early Childhood Education: A Guide for On-Site Supervision*, originally published in 1993 by the National Association for the Education of Young Children (NAEYC) and now out of print. This new book reflects changes that have occurred in the field in the intervening decades, including neuroscience research on how children learn. The book also reflects the content of two publications that are now standards for the field: *Developmentally Appropriate Practice in Early Childhood Programs Serving Children from Birth through Age 8* (2009) and *Caring for Our Children: National Health and Safety Performance Standards; Guidelines for Early Care and Education Programs*, Third Edition (2011).

While much has been written for teachers and those who work directly with children on how to support growth, development, and learning in the early years, there are relatively few resources for those who supervise early childhood programs. This book is intended to help fill that gap. It is designed as a practical tool for translating theory into practice.

Learning best practices for supporting young children and their families and how to offer and maintain high-quality early childhood education takes time and practice. For early childhood educators in all settings and roles, this learning is accomplished through working as a team to achieve high-quality programming.

In using this book, we encourage readers to begin with chapter 1, an overview of the foundations of high-quality early childhood education. This chapter offers a concise summary of what we as a field believe constitutes high quality in our diverse society.

Following this foundational chapter, the next three chapters focus on early childhood age groups:

* Chapter 2: Infants
* Chapter 3: Toddlers
* Chapter 4: Preschoolers

Each of these chapters addresses six key components of high-quality programming:

Environment: The arrangement of space, both indoors and outdoors, to ensure all children have opportunities to grow, develop, and learn

Toys, materials, and equipment: The selection and display of toys, books, and other materials that address children's developmental skills, abilities, needs, interests, home languages, cultures, and family structures

Program structure: The scheduling of daily routines, activities, and transitions to support development in all domains and provide a balanced day with opportunities to play and learn alone and with others

Curriculum: The program's written plan detailing the activities and experiences offered to promote children's growth, development, and learning

Supportive interactions: The ways in which adults communicate with and respond to children to encourage their explorations and facilitate their development in all domains

Positive guidance: Strategies for helping children learn self-regulation (that is, the ability to control bodily functions, manage emotions, and maintain focus and attention [Shonkoff and Phillips 2000]) and find acceptable ways to cope with and express strong feelings.

For each component, there are two summary charts. The first describes what you should see when visiting a high-quality program and why this practice supports children. The second identifies warning signs of potential problems, the possible reasons for the problem, and suggested solutions to implement in partnership with staff.

Chapter 5: Engaging Families, offers an overview of the important reasons for building and maintaining reciprocal partnerships with families. Such partnerships benefit children, teachers, and families. This chapter also includes summary charts, as found in chapters 2, 3, and 4.

As you read through the book, you may notice that some content is repeated in the various chapters. This is intentional. When discussing high-quality programming, certain factors need to be present in every early childhood program, whether it is designed for infants, toddlers, or preschoolers. Taking children outside daily, for instance, is such an example. In addition, content at the early childhood level is often interrelated. For example, high-quality curricula need to incorporate families as partners with teachers. Likewise, a discussion of family engagement (chapter 5) obviously hits on this same point.

Please note that throughout the book we alternate use of the terms *families, family members*, and *parents*. These terms are meant to refer to any adult who has responsibility for the child's well-being.

The following six appendixes and a listing of references complete the book:

Appendix A: A health and safety checklist that can be used to assess the environment and the toys/materials/equipment in early childhood center-based programs

Appendixes B–D: Age-specific checklists on characteristics of a high-quality environment, inventory of toys/materials/equipment, program schedule, curriculum, supportive interactions, and positive guidance in high-quality early childhood programs

Appendix E: A checklist for engaging families

Appendix F: Relevant associations, books, websites, and other resources for early childhood educators who oversee programs

Consider this book an on-the-job tool that supports your work. The content is meant to be an introduction and is by no means exhaustive. Instead, look to this book to focus your thinking and spark creative ideas and approaches for supporting the professional development of teachers. All of us in the field share the desire to provide programs for children and families that reflect the highest standards of quality. *High-Quality Early Childhood Programs: The What, Why, and How* will help you guide teachers and other staff in achieving that goal.

Foundations for Quality

In the United States, young children and families are served by a diverse early childhood education system. Diversity is characteristic of the children and families, staff, program funders and operators, and teacher preparation programs.

Child development programs are funded in a variety of ways through local, state, and federal resources and through tuition paid by families. There are full- and part-day programs serving infants, toddlers, and/or preschoolers, some operating all year as child care settings and others operating during the typical school year only. Some programs are free for families who meet certain criteria, while others are completely funded by families. For example, center-based program types include the following:

☀ public and private child care programs (for profit and not-for-profit)

☀ Early Head Start and Head Start

☀ prekindergarten, state and locally funded; often housed in elementary schools

☀ child development programs such as nursery schools and parent co-ops

☀ on-site programs for employees

☀ religion-affiliated child care

☀ military child development programs and Department of Defense pre-K and Sure Start

Diversity is also evident in teacher preparation routes and in the educational and experience requirements for teachers. In some states, licensing regulations indicate that a high school diploma is sufficient to become an early childhood education teacher, while other entities require a bachelor's degree. Teacher preparation programs include two- and four-year college and university programs, the Child Development Associate credential from the Council for Professional Recognition, high school child development courses, and on-the-job training provided by employers.

Nevertheless, high-quality programs do have characteristics in common. A visitor to such a program might not know immediately what makes the program so good, but an engaging environment, the children's joy in learning, and the teachers' caring demeanor are signs that this program has an intentional plan for excellence based on accepted standards of quality.

Standards of Quality

The quality of an early childhood program can be determined, in part, by the degree to which it meets established standards. High-quality programs reflect applicable standards for children's learning, program operations, health and safety, teacher preparation, ongoing professional development, and family engagement. Typically, these standards come from several sources and program administrators, and staff share responsibility for meeting them.

Early Learning Standards

State early learning standards or guidelines cover the skills and knowledge young children of a certain age and stage of development are expected to achieve. All states and the Department of Defense Education Activity (DoDEA) have issued standards that address the early years. The US Department of Education (2011) defines early learning and developmental standards as

> a set of expectations, guidelines, or developmental milestones that describe what all children from birth until kindergarten entry should know and be able to do and their disposition toward learning. The standards must be appropriate for each age group of infants, toddlers, and preschoolers and English learners, and for children with developmental delays and disabilities. In addition, the standards must cover all the Essential Domains of School Readiness, and must be developmentally, linguistically, and culturally appropriate.

The Department of Education goes on to define the essential domains of school readiness as "language and literacy development, cognition and general knowledge (including early mathematics and early scientific development), approaches toward learning, physical well-being and motor development, and social and emotional development."

Teachers, supervisors, and other early childhood education professionals need to be familiar with their state's early learning standards so they can apply them in their work with young children. Learning standards serve multiple purposes. They provide an overview of child development, serve as a resource for sharing information with families, guide the selection of teaching approaches and strategies, and offer benchmarks for learning and development in all domains. Find links to state early learning standards and guidelines at https://childcareta.acf.hhs.gov/resource/state-early-learning-standards-and-guidelines.

The Head Start Early Learning Outcomes Framework (ELOF) also describes what children do and learn in the early years. The ELOF was developed for use by Early Head Start and Head Start programs; however, the content is applicable to all child development programs. The framework shows the continuum of learning for infants, toddlers, and preschoolers in domains most closely related to later success in school. The domains addressed include approaches to learning, social and emotional development, language and literacy, cognition, and perceptual, motor, and physical development. Early Head

Start and Head Start programs must use the ELOF as a guide to plan teaching strategies and environments, establish goals for children in preparation for school, choose curricula and assessments, plan and offer professional development, and guide program planning, improvement, and implementation. English and Spanish versions of the ELOF and supplemental resources are available online at https://eclkc.ohs.acf.hhs.gov/school-readiness /article/head-start-early-learning-outcomes-framework.

Early Childhood Program Standards

The largest system for accrediting individual programs is administered by the National Association for the Education of Young Children. NAEYC's accreditation standards are based on child development research and best practices in programs serving infants through kindergarten-age children and define what the NAEYC believes all early childhood programs should provide. Quality criteria are organized within ten standards: relationships, curriculum, teaching, assessment of child progress, health, teachers, families, community relationships, physical environment, and leadership and management. As when addressing early learning standards, going through the accreditation process is a shared responsibility among program administrators and staff. Learn more about NAEYC's accreditation of early learning programs at www.naeyc.org/academy.

Professional Preparation Standards

NAEYC has also issued Standards for Early Childhood Professional Preparation. They are designed to cover a range of early childhood roles and settings and apply to professional preparation for higher education degree levels from associate's to BA or BS to graduate studies. Here are the six standards issued by NAEYC (2009, 11–17):

1. **Promoting Child Development and Learning.** Educators need to acquire a solid child development knowledge base.

2. **Building Family and Community Relationships.** Educators learn to develop reciprocal relationships with families and communities. Educators involve all families in their children's development and learning.

3. **Observing, Documenting, and Assessing to Support Young Children and Families.** Educators build the skills needed to conduct observations, document learning, and use other forms of assessment to keep track of and address children's development, strengths, and needs.

4. **Using Developmentally Effective Approaches to Connect with Children and Families.** Educators gain the ability to use developmentally appropriate practice to support children's development and build positive relationships with families.

5. **Using Content Knowledge to Build Meaningful Curriculum.** Educators learn how to plan and implement strategies for incorporating content disciplines in the early childhood curriculum.

6. **Becoming a Professional.** Early childhood educators accept their roles as members of an important profession who uphold standards and advocate for use of best practices to support young children.

For more information about NAEYC Standards for Early Childhood Professional Preparation, go to www.naeyc.org/files/naeyc/files/2009%20Professional%20Prep%20stds Revised%204_12.pdf.

Ethical Behavior

When supporting teachers or analyzing your own practice, you may have occasions when an ethical dilemma arises; for example, a situation where a family asks you or a teacher to do something she believes will harm the child, such as preventing the child from playing with certain classmates or depriving the child of lunch as punishment. The NAEYC Code of Ethical Conduct, Supplement for Early Childhood Program Administrators, and Supplement for Early Childhood Adult Educators offer guidelines for responsible behavior and set forth a common basis for resolving the principal ethical dilemmas encountered in early childhood care and education. The code begins with the following principle:

> Principles P-1.1—Above all, we shall not harm children. We shall not participate in practices that are emotionally damaging, physically harmful, disrespectful, degrading, dangerous, exploitative, or intimidating to children. This principle has precedence over all others in this Code. (NAEYC 2011, 3)

Often, as in the example above, this principle is sufficient to guide an educator in determining next steps. The full text of the code can be read online at www.naeyc.org /positionstatements/ethical_conduct.

Characteristics of High-Quality Early Childhood Programs

The authors of this book believe that in addition to standards set by various early childhood professional entities, a high-quality early childhood program has the following characteristics.

The Program Is Developmentally Appropriate

When a program is based on child development theory, individual child characteristics, and cultural values, it is considered developmentally appropriate. As defined by NAEYC, a developmentally appropriate program is one that is planned and carried out based on knowledge of how children grow and what they can do—socially, emotionally, cognitively, and physically—at each stage of development. Effective early childhood teachers apply their knowledge of child development and of individual children to set goals for development and learning and to plan specific strategies to help children achieve these goals. Teachers aim for goals they believe will challenge children but also allow for success. Teachers also consider what is of importance to families and valued in their cultures. The three core considerations of developmentally appropriate practice include applying knowledge about the following:

- ❋ child development and learning

- ❋ what is individually appropriate

- ❋ what is culturally important

Thus, a developmentally appropriate program addresses the unique characteristics of each child, including the child's family structure, home language, and culture. Teachers apply their knowledge of the principles of child development while using a variety of strategies to address all developmental domains through a program that supports all the children in the group. The NAEYC position statement on developmentally appropriate practice is available online at www.naeyc.org/files/naeyc/file/positions/PSDAP.pdf.

The Program Is Individualized

Although a developmentally appropriate program is, by definition, individualized, this characteristic is important enough to be further emphasized. When a child development program individualizes, it ensures that the environment; toys, materials, and equipment; program structure; curriculum; supportive interactions; and positive guidance will support the growth, development, and learning of every child in the group. Teachers use their knowledge of child development in conjunction with what they know about each child to plan a daily program that reflects the interests, cultures, skills, needs, and home languages of all children. Although most children go through a consistent sequence in their development of skills and understandings, the rate at which children progress through these stages may differ considerably. Individualizing accommodates these differing schedules.

Individualizing begins with getting to know each child and family. In a high-quality program, teachers use a variety of strategies to learn as much as they can about each child and family. They conduct home visits, provide an orientation, exchange information with families, observe children's daily interactions and activities, and document what children do, say, and learn using checklists, anecdotal records, and portfolios that collect samples of children's work. And, of course, they spend much of their time listening, talking with, and responding to children's verbal and nonverbal communications. They use what they learn to add specific items to the environment, plan activities, and devise strategies to help each child make progress.

One of the easiest ways to individualize a program is to stock the environment with engaging toys and materials, plan a variety of developmentally appropriate activities every day, and allow children to choose what they want to do and play with. The materials, interactions, and activities in a quality program should reflect what makes each child a unique individual. For example, an infant room should include a safety mirror and laminated pictures attached to the walls or floor where crawlers will notice them. It should also display visuals at a higher level where new walkers can see them.

The Program Applies Knowledge
of Young Children's Brain Development

In the late 1990s, researchers, educators, and the media highlighted what was then relatively new information about the critical importance of supporting early brain development. High-quality early childhood programs study and apply this knowledge to their practices and encourage families to provide the kinds of experiences that support brain development.

Babies are born with most of their brain cells, or neurons, already formed. The connections between the neurons, called synapses, support further brain development. Children's early experiences with the people, things, and events in their environment stimulate the development of synapses that connect with thousands of other neurons. When experiences are repeated—for example, when children hear their parents' voices—these connections are reinforced and become permanent brain pathways. When these experiences are not repeated, the connections are pruned and disappear. The brain is more flexible in the early years than at any other time of life.

In healthy environments, a child's brain grows rapidly during the early years. By the time a typical child is age two, the brain has formed 1,000 trillion connections and they are at their highest density. By age three, the brain's structure and design are almost complete. Brain connections continue to grow throughout life, but never at this same level.

Applying brain research to early childhood settings begins with understanding what adults need to do to foster optimal brain development in children's early years. What children need most is responsive care, engaging experiences, opportunities to create and explore interests, and encouragement to develop new skills and acquire knowledge. The Center on the Developing Child at Harvard University (2007) notes the following policy implications that also apply to early childhood settings:

- ☀ "Early preventive intervention will be more efficient and produce more favorable outcomes than remediation later in life." For example, an attentive teacher of toddlers notes when a child's language development appears to be stalled and shares this information with the family so they can be alert to potential problems that should be addressed now rather than later.

- ☀ "A balanced approach to emotional, social, cognitive, and language development will best prepare all children for success in school and later in the workplace and community." For example, the program implements a curriculum and uses assessment tools that address and monitor progress in all developmental domains.

- ☀ Very young children's brains require "stable, caring, interactive relationships with adults." For example, a program ensures that every infant has a primary caregiver who is the "resident expert" about the child.

- ☀ The long-term effects of toxic stress can be alleviated through specialized early interventions that "target the cause of the stress and protect the child from its consequences." For example, the program offers ongoing training, provided by mental health specialists who serve as advisers to the staff, on recognizing the signs of stress in young children.

When a child experiences nurturing, consistent, and predictable care at home and in the early childhood setting, the child's brain foundation is likely to be sturdy. However, when interactions and experiences do not respond to the child's needs, the foundation is likely to be fragile. In either case, the foundation affects emotional, social, cognitive, and language development in the early years and beyond. Understanding that the early years are a crucial time for brain development is critical for families and educators.

The Program Reflects and Values Diverse Cultures and Home Languages

Once again, although the importance of culture is one of the core considerations of developmentally appropriate practice, this characteristic deserves its own discussion. High-quality programs integrate culture and home languages in all that they do. The teachers use multiple sources—including children's families—to learn about the families' cultural values and preferences. They include artifacts and displays that are culturally relevant and provide English and home language versions of environmental print, signs, books, and messages sent home or posted on the web. Staff consult with families about fruits, vegetables, and other foods children enjoy at home and ask family members to join the class to cook or to share a favorite recipe. Each learning center reflects children's cultures and languages, including recorded music and rhythm instruments in the music and movement center. Group times are used to learn songs and fingerplays that are popular in different countries and cultures. Teachers learn how to correctly pronounce each child's name and a few important words and phrases in children's home languages. In short, teachers do their best to make the setting feel as secure and supportive as the children's homes.

The Environment Is Safe and Healthy

A quality program ensures that children are safe while they are away from their family members. This means that the adults continually check the indoor and outdoor play areas to be sure no hazards exist so children can freely explore and move around without endangering themselves or others. It also means that children are supervised at all times to prevent accidents and that adults respond immediately to any emergencies.

Children's health is a primary concern in quality programs. Staff follow standardized procedures for diapering, toileting, hand washing, and food service. Adults follow good nutrition practices in planning and serving snacks and meals and eat with children family-style to make mealtime a social and enjoyable period of the day. Children are involved in preparing snacks and meals and in cooking activities.

Standards for health and safety in early childhood programs are issued by state licensing agencies and governing and funding sources, such as Head Start and military child development programs, and from organizations with specific expertise. The American Academy of Pediatrics, American Public Health Association, and the National Resource Center for Health and Safety in Child Care and Early Education have issued *Caring for Our Children: National Health and Safety Performance Standards; Guidelines for Early Care and Education Programs,* Third Edition. This comprehensive publication includes 686 standards. It is available as a free download at http://cfoc.nrckids.org.

The Administration for Children and Families has condensed and summarized this publication into what they call the basics of health and safety. This resource was developed as a voluntary guide for states and other entities in improving licensing standards and quality improvement systems. *Caring for Our Children Basics: Health and Safety Foundations for Early Care and Education* is available online at https://www.acf.hhs.gov /sites/default/files/ecd/caring_for_our_children_basics.pdf.

Information on maintaining safe outdoor playgrounds is available from the National Program for Playground Safety at the University of Northern Iowa. Visit their website for up-to-date guidance and resources: www.playgroundsafety.org.

Children Spend Much of Their Time Learning through Play

Play is the foundation for learning and later academic success. Stefanie Adamson-Kain (2014, 22), a teacher at the Center for Young Children on the University of Maryland College Park campus, defines play in this way:

> Play is the work of young children. It comes naturally to all children, all over the world. Children are born to play. Play is a right. It expands children's creativity. It provides practice of adult roles. Play is motivating. Free play allows children time to investigate, think, socialize, question, and problem solve, without judgment from adults. Play involves risk. What will happen if I step here? What will she do if I tell her no? How do these things fit together? Why isn't this working the way I want it to? Play allows children to express themselves as artists, mathematicians, scientists, athletes, readers, writers, caretakers, leaders, and so much more. It builds confidence so that children will feel comfortable as they encounter challenges throughout their lives.

High-quality early childhood programs are play-based. Teachers use a variety of strategies to support learning, including short periods of direct instruction when appropriate, but facilitating children's play is a primary strategy. Facilitating play includes asking questions, making suggestions, inviting children to describe and explain, and involving children in defining and solving problems. It also includes providing what children need to play—time, toys and materials, a safe setting, encouragement, and guidance on developing social skills essential for playing with others.

Children Have Many Opportunities to Make Choices as They Engage in Active Learning

Quality programs help children develop independence and view themselves as competent learners. Toys and materials are kept on low shelves where children can reach what they need and learn to return them when they are finished. Giving children choices helps them learn to make decisions and ensures that they can participate in activities that interest them. Children learn best when they can explore concrete materials and when they can share their ideas and questions with other children and with caring adults. In a quality program, you will see children who are involved and active and who are talking and playing freely with others.

Choices are not limited to materials and activities, however. In a high-quality program, teachers engage children in making other age-appropriate decisions, such as deciding how much food to put on their plates or which book to read at group time. They also apply this concept to positive guidance, offering children acceptable alternatives to certain behaviors. To a child who is having trouble paying attention at group time, a teacher might say, "It's not okay to run around the room during story time. You can play with a toy from the fidget basket while you listen to the story or you can work on a puzzle at the table with Mr. Ken."

Adults Show Respect for Children's Needs and Ideas and Interact with Them in Caring Ways

High-quality programs implement relationship-based care and teaching. The quality of the program is most evident in the ways that adults build relationships with children. Adults respond quickly to children's needs and communications. Infants and toddlers need adults who will hold them, soothe them, and provide caring attention to ensure their emotional and physical comfort. As children get older, they thrive around adults who will listen to their ideas, respond to their questions, and help them learn to think for themselves.

Young children are building self-regulation skills as they learn what behavior is acceptable and what is not acceptable. Over time they will become better at coping with impulses and learn to wait rather than acting on urges. They need adults who will guide their behavior in positive ways that build self-esteem. This means not punishing children, belittling them, or yelling at them when they make mistakes but rather setting clear and consistent limits. Adults patiently explain the rules to children—as often as needed, redirect them to acceptable behavior, and help them learn to solve problems on their own.

Positive interactions also support learning as teachers observe and listen carefully to children's actions and communications. Effective teachers ask open-ended questions that do not have right or wrong answers, allowing children to progress to higher levels of thinking. They might repeat what a child says to ensure the message received is the one the child meant to send. They narrate a child's actions to help a child pay attention to the steps he or she takes to complete a task or join a group at play.

Programs Encourage Meaningful, Reciprocal Family Engagement

In quality programs, families and staff are partners on a team devoted to supporting a child's development and learning. Most parents have known their children since birth and are firsthand witnesses to their child's activities and behaviors in the family setting. They can share valuable information about their child's experiences at home with teachers, who also share valuable information about the child's experiences at the program. Such information exchanges take place frequently. The younger the child, the more often families and teachers communicate. For example, parents of infants want to know such news every day, while parents of older children may be comfortable with weekly updates.

Teachers have specialized training in child development and early childhood education and have experience guiding the learning of many children. They see children living and learning among their peers. In quality programs, teachers greet family members by name, take time to talk about the program and their children's progress, invite parents to participate in activities or special events, and share resources with parents.

Teachers and families also work together to make decisions about the program, advocate for children's well-being, plan events and workshops, and create a welcoming community for all enrolled children and families. When parents and staff understand how important it is to exchange information and work together, children benefit most from their experience.

All Program Staff—Regardless of Role, Education, or Experience—Pursue Professional Learning

In high-quality early childhood programs, all staff are lifelong learners. A teacher's professional journey may include receiving a Child Development Associate (CDA) credential, graduating from community college, and pursuing undergraduate and graduate degrees. Regardless, there is always something new to learn, and continually working to keep up with the latest knowledge and skills in the field is essential to being an excellent teacher.

Supporting the professional development of staff may be one of your responsibilities. You may authorize funds for tuition reimbursement, arrange for on-site workshops, or include time in the schedule for teachers to take online courses. In addition, you will visit classrooms to observe teachers and children in action. Thus, you must maintain excellent and effective observation skills that provide clear, objective information about a teacher's strategies and how children respond.

Part of your role is to build relationships with individual teachers, to identify and build on their strengths, and often, to serve as a coach. Here's how coaching is defined by NAEYC and the National Association for Child Care Resource and Referral Agencies (NACCRRA—now known as Child Care Aware of America) in their *Early Childhood Education Professional Development: Training and Technical Assistance Glossary*:

> Coaching is a relationship-based process led by an expert with specialized and adult learning knowledge and skills, who often serves in a different professional role than the recipient(s). Coaching is designed to build capacity for specific professional dispositions, skills, and behaviors and is focused on goal-setting and achievement for an individual or group. (NAEYC and NACCRRA 2011, 11)

It is also important to note that "collaborative relationships and ongoing observation and conversation are central to the success of coaching" (Jablon, Dombro, and Johnsen 2014, 13).

Many funding agencies require early education program staff to write their own annual professional development plans in collaboration with supervisors and trainers. The plan serves as a road map, outlining how the individual will gain and apply desired skills and knowledge in the coming year. Plans are based on individual and program needs and interests. For example, a teacher might want to learn more about supporting science learning—a goal that dovetails with the program's goal of enhancing the science curriculum by providing children with greater opportunities to explore the natural world.

Teachers Have Knowledge and Skills and the Disposition to Be Early Childhood Educators

Laura J. Colker surveyed a variety of early childhood educators to find out what attracted them to the field of early childhood education, the skills needed, the challenges they faced, and the rewards they reaped. Based on these responses, she defined the following twelve characteristics of effective teachers (Colker 2008, 3–5):

1. **Passion.** Probably more than anything else, teachers report that it's important to have a passion for what you do. . . . Being an early childhood educator is not always easy. There may be physical and financial challenges, for example. But if you feel that what you are doing makes a difference, that sense of accomplishment can sustain and motivate you.

2. **Perseverance.** [Perseverance is] the willingness to fight for one's beliefs, whether related to children's needs or education issues. Teachers have to be willing to be long-term advocates for improving the lives of children and their families. . . . Children need and deserve teachers who can overcome bureaucracy and handle red tape.

3. **Willingness to take risks.** Successful educators are willing to shake up the status quo to achieve goals for children. Great teachers are willing to go against the norm. Taking a risk means not settling for a no answer if a yes will improve the quality of a child's education.

4. **Pragmatism.** Pragmatists are willing to compromise. They know which battles are winnable and when to apply their resources in support of children. . . . Effective teachers understand that by temporarily settling for small wins, they are still making progress toward their goals.

5. **Patience.** In line with pragmatism is the characteristic of patience. . . . Not every child learns quickly. Some behaviors can challenge even the most effective teacher. . . . Good teachers have a long fuse for exasperation, frustration, and anger.

6. **Flexibility.** Early childhood education demands that you be able to deal well with change and unexpected turns. Whether it's raining outside and you have to cancel outdoor play, or your funding agency has drastically reduced your operating budget, you need to be able to switch gears at a moment's notice and find an alternative that works.

7. **Respect.** Respect for children and families is basic to being a good early childhood teacher. [Respect includes] an appreciation for diversity . . . and the belief that everyone's life is enhanced by exposure to people of different backgrounds who speak a variety of languages. . . . Good teachers create this environment naturally.

8. **Creativity.** It takes creativity to teach in a physical environment that is less than ideal or when resources are limited. It takes creativity to teach children from diverse backgrounds who might not approach education in the same way. . . . And most of all, it takes creativity to make learning fun.

9. **Authenticity.** Being authentic means knowing who you are and what you stand for. It is what gives you integrity and conviction. Young children are shrewd judges of character; they know whether a teacher is authentic, and they respond accordingly.

10. **Love of learning.** To inspire children with a love of learning . . . teachers themselves ought to exhibit this characteristic. Teachers who are lifelong learners send children the message that learning is an important part of life. . . . Being an effective teacher involves seeking out knowledge about recent research on teaching.

11. **High energy.** Most children respond positively to teachers with high energy levels, valuing their enthusiasm.

12. **Sense of humor.** Learning should be fun; nothing conveys this message more than a room that is filled with spontaneous laughter.

As you perform your daily work and collaborate with teachers to ensure that your program is serving children and families well, keep these standards for quality in mind. Adopt or adapt the characteristics of high-quality early childhood programs to fit your situation. Knowing what you want to accomplish with your program will keep you focused on your goals.

BLOCK
AREA

2 Ensuring the Effectiveness of Infant Programs

High-quality infant programs provide a warm and homelike environment to help children feel comfortable, secure, and eager to explore and learn. Teachers meet infants' needs consistently, promptly, and lovingly, while responding to each child's individual schedule. This means that children are fed when hungry, changed when their diapers are wet or soiled, comforted when they are distressed, and placed in their cribs when they are sleepy. Teachers talk, read, sing, and engage children throughout the day. Teachers hold and comfort infants using methods suggested by the children's families. They offer infants frequent opportunities to play on the floor or in a large, protected crawl area. Teachers also encourage infants to use their senses and their rapidly growing physical and cognitive skills to explore the indoor and outdoor environments.

You can use the information and guidance in this chapter to oversee the environment, the toys, materials, and equipment, the program structure, the curriculum, supportive interactions, and positive guidance. Some of the examples in this chapter refer to infants as *young* or *mobile*. Young infants are children from birth to nine months old, and mobile infants are children from eight to eighteen months. The overlapping months allow for the wide variation in individual children's rates of growth, development, and learning.

This chapter includes the following sections:

☀ Environment, pages 20–26

☀ Toys, Materials, and Equipment, pages 27–33

☀ Program Structure, pages 34–39

☀ Curriculum: Activities and Experiences, pages 40–45

☀ Supportive Interactions, pages 45–50

☀ Positive Guidance, pages 51–55

Environment

The starting point for overseeing and maintaining a high-quality infant program is having a physical environment that is designed and arranged to facilitate children's growth, development, and learning. Indeed, the program design is a blueprint for curriculum implementation. It also creates a physical and social atmosphere that reflects your program's philosophy and enables teachers to support individual and group progress.

Foundations Underlying Quality

Before observing the effectiveness of the program environment, you will need to be sure certain baseline standards for quality are being met. These standards include the size of the indoor and outdoor settings, health and safety measures, and how the setting is arranged to support children, teachers, and families.

Program Space

Infant programs are housed in a wide variety of dedicated or adapted spaces, ranging from classrooms to trailers to church facilities. Standards for indoor space are set by federal (in the case of Early Head Start and military child development), state, local, and tribal licensing authorities and vary, so you need to check the square footage requirements of your own licensing agency or other governing body. Early Head Start programs, for example, have to comply with state, tribal, or local licensing regulations but must provide a minimum of thirty-five square feet per child, exclusive of space for cribs and diaper-changing areas (Office of Head Start 2017).

Because the size of the space directly correlates with quality, exceeding these requirements can benefit children. *Caring for Our Children*, a compilation of health and safety performance standards issued jointly by the American Academy of Pediatrics, the American Public Health Association, and the National Resource Center for Health and Safety in Child Care and Early Education, notes that "historically, a standard of thirty-five square feet was used. Recommendations from research studies range between forty-two to fifty-four square feet per child. . . . Child behavior tends to be more constructive when sufficient space is organized to promote developmentally appropriate skills. Crowding has been shown to be associated with increased risk of developing upper respiratory infections. Also, having sufficient space will reduce the risk of injury from simultaneous activities" (American Academy of Pediatrics 2011, 203). *Caring for Our Children* recommends a minimum of forty-two square feet per child but states that fifty square feet of usable floor space is "preferred" (American Academy of Pediatrics 2011).

The space designated for outdoor play and learning includes soil, sand, grass, hills, and flat, hard surfaces. Federal, state, local, and tribal regulations on appropriate square footage for outdoor environments vary. However, *Caring for Our Children* recommends at least thirty-three square feet of accessible outdoor play space per mobile infant (American Academy of Pediatrics 2011).

Health and Safety

Before supervisors can effectively monitor how the environment supports children and teachers, they must check the setting to ensure it is a safe and healthy place for children's play, routines, and experiences. Making sure nothing unsafe or unhealthy is within reach can be especially challenging for those supervising infant programs, as infants spend so much time on the floor or the ground. Your local, state, or tribal licensing agency issues mandatory health and safety guidelines. Early Head Start and military child development programs have stringent standards for health and safety requirements.

To ensure that the environment of your program complies with indoor and outdoor health and safety requirements, we have included a checklist in appendix A. Though not all-inclusive, this checklist reflects Early Head Start and military child development program regulations. Once you are assured that children are safe and healthy, you can concentrate on how the environment facilitates infants' growth, development, and learning.

Room / Outdoor Space Arrangement

Best practices in the infant years include arranging the setting into spaces to accommodate children's routines and learning experiences. A well-planned and supportive setting for infants includes the following:

* a family greeting space where family members and teachers can communicate and exchange information about each child's daily routines and activities at home and at the program

* cubbies for storing personal items from home

* a private nursing/feeding area for mothers to feed their babies and teachers to give babies bottles

* protected floor space for "tummy time" and reaching for, dropping, throwing, and exploring objects

* space for playing with books, toys, water, mirrors, and sensory items

* a well-stocked diapering area

* an area with cribs for sleeping

* an area for eating with low chairs with trays (for young infants who can sit independently)

For mobile infants, designate additional space for the following activities:

* eating meals and snacks and having tasting experiences at child-size chairs with trays or at child-size tables and chairs

* crawling, standing, walking, and moving about

* exploring and pushing toys

* filling and dumping blocks, clothespins, beanbags, and other objects into and out of containers

☀ rolling balls

☀ playing with sand and water

An appropriate environment for infants looks a lot like a home. There are spaces where teachers can spend time getting to know individual infants. There are a variety of levels and textures to explore.

Outdoor places for young infants require little more than soft, grassy areas. Teachers can place a blanket or carpet square on the grass, and children can watch, listen to, and interact with people and nature. Babies also need space to roll over, crawl, pull themselves up, climb, waddle, and walk.

Mobile infants need more than the sensory exploration on which young infants thrive. The outdoor space should offer opportunities for mobile infants to do the following activities:

☀ crawl, walk, climb, and roll over

☀ use infant swings, pull-up bars, and tunnels

☀ throw and roll balls

☀ push and pull toys

☀ paint and play with water

☀ play with sand and toys in a sandbox

What the Environment Should Look Like

The most important component of the environment in the infant room are the teachers, whose positive, supportive interactions and guidance help infants grow, develop, and learn. In high-quality programs, infants are assigned a primary teacher who builds a close, reciprocal relationship with them and their families.

Following are examples of what you should see in a center-based program that serves infants and why these arrangements of the environment are important.

What you should see	Why
Cozy, homelike touches such as hanging plants, soft floor pillows, mirrors, tablecloths, rocking chairs, and items specific to the children's cultures and home languages.	Infants are developing a sense of trust. Since most babies feel secure at home with their families, re-creating a familiar homelike atmosphere that reflects the children's cultures and home languages enhances their sense of security. When children are secure and trust their environment, they feel safe enough to explore and learn. Having a familiar atmosphere also eases children's transition from home to the program and back again.
Photos of infants attending the program and their families hung at children's eye level or laminated on the floor. Safety mirrors hung at children's eye level.	Pictures and mirrors need to be hung low enough for children to see them on their own. Laminated pictures affixed to the floor are readily viewed by young infants and crawlers. Family photos help infants cope with being separated from loved ones. They can "check in" with family members throughout the day. Looking at themselves in the mirror or in photos helps children develop a sense of self and feel valued.
Soft (carpeted), protected areas in which to sit, creep, crawl, walk, and push wheeled toys and cars.	Infants have an inborn need to move and explore their environment. Soft, protected places where children can fall without hurting themselves make their explorations safe and allow babies to grow and develop.
Areas with easy-to-clean flooring, such as linoleum, for messy activities like painting and water play.	Older infants need to be free to explore, experiment, and create without the constraints of having to be neat—a near impossibility at this age.
An inviting family greeting space where teachers welcome children and families, family members sit and help children put on and take off jackets and outerwear, and teachers and families exchange information about the child.	Families and teachers are partners in supporting infants' development and learning. Both families and teachers are an integral part of the infant program. Providing this area communicates that teachers and families work together to support infants' well-being.
An easily sanitized diapering area that is regularly stocked with supplies and has a foot-operated trash can lined with a plastic bag.	A well-planned diapering area where teachers have what they need at hand allows them to spend diapering time interacting with children and building reciprocal relationships.
Cribs for each child located in an open area where they are visible to teachers.	A visible napping area allows teachers to tell at a glance whether children are awake or sleeping. Teachers can respond promptly and consistently to children once they are awake. Prompt and consistent care builds a sense of trust, which in turn encourages children to feel safe and explore and learn.

What you should see	Why
Comfortable adult-size chairs or gliders available in a private spot for nursing mothers and teachers feeding bottles to young infants. There are low infant chairs with trays for young infants who can sit, and child-size tables and chairs are grouped together for mobile infants to eat together.	Adults can focus on and bond with individual infants in quiet, secluded spaces. Once infants can sit, low chairs with trays are appropriate so children can sit comfortably with their feet on the floor. Mobile infants can socialize in groups of two or three when seated at a low table in child-size chairs.
Sturdy furniture and equipment such as railings are available to infants indoors and outdoors to pull themselves up.	Infants use these supports to safely raise themselves from a sitting or crawling position to standing upright—a precursor to walking.
Culturally and developmentally appropriate toys and other learning materials (including duplicates of the children's favorites) displayed on low, open shelving.	When children can see and reach toys, they can choose what they want to use and return the items when done. Infants are not yet developmentally able to share, so having duplicates avoids frustration.
Outdoor play space for infants adjacent to but separate from where toddlers play. The space for young infants is itself protected from older, mobile children. Swings and paths for riding toys used by mobile infants are located at edges of play area. Space for noisy activities is separated from space for quiet activities.	These design features support safe outdoor play. Have separate areas for toddlers to protect infants from their always-active elders. Likewise, separate mobile infants from young infants to protect the stationary babies from being run into or tripped over. Offering swings and riding toys on the peripheral areas enables mobile infants to have fun using this equipment without disturbing more vulnerable younger infants. Separating noisy and quiet activities allows children to better focus and learn.
Storage spaces and furniture for adults (teachers, family members, visitors), including comfortable chairs or a sofa for feeding, reading to, and interacting with infants.	Adults need to be able to store their possessions where they will be safe and pose no harm to children. Comfortable, adult-size furniture encourages adults to cuddle and spend more one-on-one time with children.

When the twelve items noted above are in place, the environment is likely to support infants' growth, development, and learning. Use the checklist in appendix B to observe how well your program meets these criteria. For items that your program is not yet addressing well, work with teachers to devise and implement an action plan for improvement. As a supervisor, you are responsible for ensuring that all components of the indoor and outdoor environment are optimally serving children and teachers.

When the Environment Needs Further Adjusting

For deeper insight into the effectiveness of the environment, it's important to observe how teachers and children use the indoor and outdoor spaces. It's one thing to have a well-designed and laid out environment. However, unless children are using it as planned, it will not support the program's goals for children. If you spot children engaged in behaviors such as those described below, the environment may be contributing to problems that hamper their progress. Discuss the possible solutions noted in the third column with teachers and help them implement these countermeasures, if appropriate.

Note: Some of the warning signs listed below may be caused by factors other than the environment or by a combination of environmental and other factors. Regular observations will provide information about the actual cause of the problem.

Warning sign	Why this might be happening	How educators can address the problem
The room is filled with commercial art posters featuring popular media characters.	Since the posters are colorful and the characters are familiar, teachers think they will make the room child-friendly.	Infants are most attracted to photos of people in their world—namely, themselves and members of their families. Work with teachers to redecorate the walls, using photos hung at the children's eye level—and even some that are laminated and taped to the floor.
Mobile infants walk into and trip over young infants during play.	There are not protected places for young infants to play that are away from mobile infants in transit.	Indoors, help teachers move the furniture to provide a protected space for babies. Use soft blocks or low shelving to create a sheltered area. Outdoors, place young infants on blankets or carpet squares on grassy areas.
Children look at toys on shelves but don't take them out to play.	Materials are on high shelves, out of children's reach. Or materials are crowded together, making it difficult to choose something to play with.	Work with teachers to neatly arrange a few toys/materials on each shelf. Items should be within reach of a child on the floor.
Nursing mothers rush through feeding their child and leave as soon as possible.	The space for nursing is either not welcoming, quiet, private, or comfortable—or some combination of all these factors.	Help teachers to carve out a comfortable and private nursing area where mothers can interact and bond with their children during the nursing experience.

Warning sign	Why this might be happening	How educators can address the problem
Infants who can sit are placed in traditional high chairs for meals.	Traditional high chairs are the only option available for feeding younger infants who can sit. The only alternative is to seat children at child-size tables and chairs, which they are too small to use safely.	Traditional high chairs are not recommended for group programs because of the potential for accidents and reduced opportunities for socializing. Together with teachers, try to replace the high chairs with low-to-the-ground, child-size chairs (with seats eight to ten inches from the floor) that have attached trays. These chairs with trays are safe, promote socializing, and encourage independence, since children can sit and stand on their own. At about eleven months of age, most children are tall enough to sit in child-size chairs at low tables.
Infants who are awake remain in their cribs, as long as they don't cry.	Teachers are busy meeting the needs of other children. They believe that as long as infants are safe, it is fine to leave them unattended for a while.	Offer practical suggestions for meeting the needs of several infants at once. For example, teachers might use a front pack to hold a young infant while reading a book to another child. Model ways to pay attention to more than one child at a time, such as holding one child while rolling a ball to another.
Young infants spend all of the time outdoors in their strollers.	Teachers may not realize that babies benefit from exploring the outdoors and that they are capable of more than just watching and listening.	Work with teachers to set up an outdoor area where young infants can be on blankets and watch, listen to, observe, and interact with people, toys, and, most important, nature. Encourage teachers to carry babies around the play area, talking and pointing out the sights and sounds.
Mobile infants run around outside aimlessly "letting off steam" while teachers discuss plans for afternoon events.	The outside area is not defined and set up for mobile infants to enjoy activities such as using push-style riding toys, pushing and pulling toys, rolling and throwing balls, collecting natural items, making (and knocking down) constructions, and filling/dumping sand and water. Also, teachers don't understand that interacting with children during playtimes supports language development and other skills.	Work with teachers to set up an outdoor space that challenges and excites mobile infants. Brainstorm ways to introduce children to the different activities they can do outside. Stress to teachers the importance of supporting children's play outdoors in the same way they support indoor play.

Toys, Materials, and Equipment

The effectiveness of well-designed indoor and outdoor environments is directly dependent on how these areas are stocked with toys, materials, and equipment. High-quality infant programs contain a varied supply of homey and purchased items appropriate for the ages, stages, abilities, interests, cultures, languages, and other characteristics of the children in the group. They both match and challenge the children's wide range of skills and knowledge. Children need to experience success and, at the same time, be sufficiently challenged to learn new skills and concepts.

Foundations Underlying Quality

Before observing the equipment, toys, and materials in your program's indoor and outdoor environments to ensure their effectiveness, you will need to be sure certain baseline standards for quality are being met. These standards pertain to the developmental appropriateness of the inventory and their adherence to safety.

Selection of Toys, Materials, and Equipment

A high-quality program for infants should be stocked with items that babies can explore with all their senses. Infants are particularly prone to put everything in their mouths. Items also need to support children's burgeoning growth, development, and learning. Selecting toys, materials, and equipment for infants can be tricky because there are dramatic changes in development between young infants of two months and mobile infants of eighteen months. Therefore, programs need to offer a wide range of choices so that every child in the group has something interesting with which to play.

Because every program—and the children and families served—has unique characteristics, no one master inventory is appropriate for all infant classrooms. Your choices should reflect the cultures, home languages, and families of the children in the group, as well as your budget. In addition, if children in your program have special needs, the inventory needs to be supplemented with toys, materials, and equipment that are adapted so all children can fully participate in the program.

The following lists are in no way exhaustive. Rather, these lists are a starting point for checking that your program has an age-appropriate, individually appropriate, and culturally appropriate inventory for young and mobile infants (Dodge, Rudick, and Berke 2011).

Homey and natural

☀ pots and pans

☀ wooden spoons

☀ plastic bowls and cups

☀ unbreakable kitchen utensils and cutlery (with no sharp edges)

☀ shells (sterilized and larger than 1¾ inches in diameter)

☀ leaves

☀ plastic bottles

☀ different kinds of paper—tissue, waxed, colorful

☀ cardboard boxes with and without lids

Language and literacy

☀ cloth, plastic, and vinyl books—homemade or purchased—that are safe to mouth

☀ texture books and books that have movable parts, flaps, and holes

☀ board books

☀ pictures, mounted on cardboard and laminated

☀ cloth or rubber puppets with no removable parts

☀ photos of infants' families, familiar objects, and animals.

Sensory stimulation

☀ mobiles—homemade or purchased

☀ mirrors (unbreakable)

☀ wall hangings (textured, touchable, and securely fastened)

☀ fabric scraps of different textures

☀ clutch, textured, and weighted balls

☀ push, pull, and squeeze toys

☀ toys for sucking, chewing, and teething

☀ cuddle toys, animals, and dolls

☀ texture glove made from a variety of materials (to be worn by an adult)

☀ plastic/rubber tub or basin, or cafeteria tray for water play

☀ plastic containers, cups, bottles, and pitchers for water play

Manipulative toys

☀ peekaboo toys

☀ jack-in-the-box and other pop-up toys

☀ busy boxes and surprise boxes

☀ stacking post and rings

☀ shape-sorting boxes

☀ nesting boxes/baskets

☀ large foam and cardboard blocks

☀ stacking blocks

☀ containers in graduated sizes (such as plastic bowls or cups)

☀ pegboards with large holes and pegs

☀ puzzles with two to four pieces with knobs

Gross-motor development

☀ reaching/grasping toys

☀ soft balls of various sizes

☀ small cars, trucks, trains, and other vehicles

☀ child-size carriages/strollers, shopping carts, lawn mowers, and other wheeled push toys

☀ riding toys (without pedals) propelled by arms or feet

☀ carpeted climbers

☀ low, carpeted/cushioned risers

☀ cushioned climbing equipment in various shapes

☀ tunnels

Art

☀ large, nontoxic jumbo crayons and papers (wax, parchment, rice, tissue, cellophane)

☀ doughs and blunt, wooden dowels to use as tools

☀ fingerpaints and paper or shallow trays

☀ stubby-handled brushes

☀ jumbo chalk

☀ smocks

Music and movement

- musical mobiles
- rattles and other rhythm instruments (tambourines, maracas, clackers)
- bell bracelets and anklets
- push and pull toys that make music
- balls with bells inside them
- music boxes (to wind up or to pull)
- CD player with CDs, MP3 player, tablet, or other form of digital music (to be used by adult)
- picture book versions of songs and fingerplays

Pretend play

- dolls (soft, unbreakable, washable, and multiethnic)
- doll bottles, blankets, and cradle or crib
- stuffed animals
- hats, purses, tote bags, backpacks
- unbreakable tea set
- real or toy telephones
- child-size pots, pans, and plastic dishes and utensils

Outdoor play

- plastic containers, cups, bowls, bottles, pitchers, funnels, colanders, pails, and buckets (for sand or water play)
- shovels (child-size)
- rakes (child-size)
- watering cans
- streamers
- wind chimes / hanging crystals (out of children's reach)
- blankets and mats for young infants
- beanbags
- boxes

Indoors

- glider, rocking chair, or other adult seating
- low tables with infant-size chairs / low child-size chairs with trays
- room dividers / low, open shelving
- unbreakable mounted mirrors
- cubbies / storage units
- cribs / evacuation cribs
- child-size cutlery
- storage for adult items and for toys and materials that are used only with supervision

Outdoors

- fully enclosed infant swings
- tires (mobile infants only)
- slide
- climber
- playhouse
- water tub
- sterilized play sand and sand tub / sandbox (mobile infants only)
- buggy/strollers for taking children on walks

SAFETY REMINDERS

All the equipment, materials, and toys in your program must meet these safety requirements:

- be free of sharp edges, splinters, lead paint, and other toxins
- pose no potential choking or suffocation hazards
- meet applicable safety guidelines issued by local, state, or tribal licensing agencies, Early Head Start, or military child development programs

Use the safety checklist in appendix A to ensure that the toys, materials, and equipment in your program are appropriate for young and mobile infants.

What Toys, Materials, and Equipment Should Look Like

In a high-quality infant program, the toys, materials, and equipment in the indoor and outdoor spaces should be varied, developmentally appropriate, and inviting. In the following examples, you will see what quality measures should be in place when you observe the toys, materials, and equipment in an infant program and why these measures are important.

What you should see	Why
Items infants can suck on, chew, lick, squeeze, pinch, roll, bang, shake, smell, and observe.	Children learn through all their senses. They use their eyes, ears, noses, mouths, and hands to explore toys and materials and learn about the people and things in their world.
Toys and other materials with bright colors, interesting shapes, shiny surfaces, noisy parts, and textured coverings.	Color, texture, and noise attract young infants who are dependent on sensory explorations to learn.
Items that encourage mobile infants to move and gain gross-motor and fine-motor skills (for example, push and pull toys, balls, markers and crayons with paper, puzzles, and blocks).	Mobile infants crave materials and equipment that will help them develop their ever-increasing gross-motor skills of standing, walking, and throwing. As their hand-muscle skills develop, materials like puzzles and blocks promote eye-hand coordination.
Household items, such as plastic measuring cups, wooden spoons, and cardboard boxes.	Household items are familiar to infants. Being reminded of home strengthens their sense of security.
Open-ended toys, materials, and equipment (for example, items that can be used in a variety of different ways, such as balls and dolls).	Open-ended toys and equipment can be explored in new and exciting ways as infants mature and develop new skills. Because there is no one right way to use these toys and materials, different children can use them in unique ways.
Natural materials to explore and manipulate, such as water, leaves, pinecones, and sand (for mobile infants only).	Sensory experiences with natural items are soothing. They also promote cognitive development as children observe what happens after they splash water or crumble a leaf.
Materials that encourage pretending and taking on roles (for example, a telephone, dress-up props, or baby dolls with cribs).	By about fifteen months, mobile infants can remember actions and imitate them later on. This is the beginning of pretend play. Props like phones and hats help children extend play and develop thinking skills.

What you should see	Why
Washable books in English and children's home languages with simple pictures that focus on familiar things and have repetitive language or rhymes, or are wordless.	It is never too early to read with a child. Reading to children from the time they are newborns provides a foundation for social and emotional development and language and literacy. As adults read aloud, infants begin to connect reading with warm feelings, and language and print with images. Books introduce children to exciting places, things, and people.
Materials that encourage problem solving and other cognitive skills (for example, pegboards, puzzles, shape sorters, and stacking rings).	Infants develop thinking skills as they explore objects and see how they work. When they empty a surprise box and out falls a stuffed dragonfly, they gain a beginning understanding of cause and effect.
Materials that promote the visual arts and music (for example, bell bracelets, chimes, cloud dough, and jumbo crayons).	Art appreciation begins as young infants turn their heads toward music and are calmed or excited by the type of sounds they hear. Mobile infants respond to music physically and can sing and play instruments. Young infants enjoy the sensory experience of feeling the texture of fabrics and of papers. Mobile infants can fingerpaint, use a brush to paint a wall with water, draw, and mold dough.
Unbreakable, child-size plates, bowls, cups, forks, and spoons.	Mobile infants develop independence, self-esteem, and pride by being able to feed themselves. Child-size, durable cutlery promotes this independence. Mobile infants can learn to feed themselves, first with their hands, then with a spoon or two, and ultimately with a fork used as a spear.
Equipment and materials outdoors that promote gross-motor activity and interaction with nature (for example, swings, slides, climbers, sand and water tubs/boxes, a playhouse, and a garden).	Infants need to be outdoors every day to experience sensory and physical development. Mobile infants require open spaces and equipment to develop their large muscles. All infants benefit from being in the wind and sun and from observing plants, flowers, trees, bugs, birds, and worms.

When you observe the twelve items noted above in place, it is likely that the equipment and materials in your program support infants' learning. Use the checklist in appendix B to observe how well your program meets these criteria. For items that your program is not yet addressing well, work with teachers to devise and implement an action plan for improvement. As a supervisor, you have the important role of ensuring that program toys, materials, and equipment optimally support children's growth, development, and learning.

When the Toys, Materials, and Equipment Need Further Adjusting

For deeper insight into the effectiveness of your program's equipment and materials, it's important to observe children and teachers using the materials. It's one thing to have a well-thought-out inventory of safe and developmentally appropriate toys, materials, and equipment. However, unless children and teachers are using these items in ways that facilitate children's growth, development, and learning, they are of little use. If you spot behaviors such as those described below, the equipment, toys, and materials may be contributing to problems that hamper learning. Discuss with teachers the warning sign, reasons why the behavior might be happening, and the possible solutions noted in the third column. Help them implement these countermeasures or others they develop to make your program's toys, materials, and equipment more effective.

Note: Some of the warning signs listed below may be caused by factors other than the program's equipment, toys, and materials or by a combination of the program's equipment, toys, and materials and other factors. Regular observations will provide information about the precise cause of the problem.

Warning sign	Why this might be happening	How educators can address the problem
Children seem uninterested in the toys, materials, and equipment available for their use.	Children are bored because the toys, materials, and equipment are one-dimensional (have only one use) or too complex. Or items are not displayed so they are engaging and accessible to infants.	Work with teachers to make sure they offer items that match the abilities, interests, and other characteristics of each child in the group. Because babies develop so quickly, a broad range of playthings is needed to meet everyone's needs. Ensure that playthings are displayed on low shelving that children can access.
Infants fight over popular playthings.	Teachers think that it is important to learn about sharing in the early years. They do not know that babies are not yet ready to develop the skills needed to be able to share.	Emphasize to teachers that infants are not developmentally capable of sharing. Have them keep track of which items are used most often so they can offer duplicates (or triplicates) of popular items. This will avoid many disagreements among infants.
Books and popular toys are stored on high shelves that only adults can reach.	Teachers are afraid that children will destroy the materials, or teachers want to control the flow of toys since infants aren't able to share popular items.	Children learn best when they can independently take out a toy they want to use. Help teachers display the materials so children can see what is available and take out toys without having to ask an adult to help.

Warning sign	Why this might be happening	How educators can address the problem
Balls and other items taken outdoors are stored in the water table, near the outside exit.	Teachers find it easy to store things in the water table. If the table is full, they won't need to offer indoor water play, which can be messy and requires close supervision.	Help teachers identify another place to store outdoor play materials. An outdoor shed is one good solution. Once the water tub is available, observe to see it has been set up for children's use. If not, visit the classroom to model how to set up and supervise water play. Then discuss what the children did and learned from the experience.
Young infants give up and cry when trying to stack rings on cones or when using shape sorters.	The toys are too advanced for the children's developmental levels and cause frustration.	Work with teachers to ensure that there are toys and other materials that each child can master. Underscore the importance of each child experiencing success. Suggest that teachers provide open-ended toys, where there are no "right" solutions.
Teacher-made "All about Me" books have torn and crumpled pages.	The books are made with paper that is too thin to stand the wear and tear and mouthings of infant readers.	Hold a workshop on making infant books. Stress the need to "babyproof" the books by making them out of cardboard, poster board, or oilcloth, or by laminating the pages. Provide materials so participants can make books during the workshop. Explain that even these sturdy books may need to be replaced after a few months of use.
Mobile infants do not choose to do puzzles or use pegboards and other manipulatives.	Children may have already mastered the materials, so now they are too simple and uninteresting. Teachers have not observed regularly and therefore have not rotated the materials they offer to children.	Because children gain skills so quickly in infancy, materials need to be rotated often to reflect their growing skills. Likewise, materials should respond to children's current interests.
Outdoors, mobile infants run after balls but have difficulty picking them up and playing with them.	The balls are too small for children to grasp, which can lead to frustration.	Ask teachers to think about what infants are doing with the balls. Explain that mobile infants develop physical skills by holding, dropping, rolling, and throwing balls they can grasp with both hands. Beach balls and large playground balls work best for young children just learning these skills.

Program Structure

The program structure in an infant setting revolves around individual needs. To a certain extent, there is a sequence of events—eating, napping, being changed and dressed, playing with toys, being read to, going outdoors, and exploring the environment—that offers predictability to the day. However, the order and timing of events is dictated by each infant's unique body clock. With young infants, the schedule completely conforms to children's bodily needs. With mobile infants, a routine such as having lunch or snack can be done in small groups to encourage socialization.

Foundations Underlying Quality

Before observing your program's structure to ensure its effectiveness, you will need to be sure your program's schedule is appropriate for caring for infants.

Sample Schedule for an Infant Program

Infant rooms have wholly flexible schedules so that teachers can meet the individual needs of each child. Generally the schedule indicates arrival and departure times, indoor and outdoor playtimes, and meal- and naptimes. Routines make up the bulk of the infants' days and are, therefore, the most important events on the schedule. Teachers take advantage of routines such as diapering, feeding, washing, and dressing to build relationships with infants, get to know them as unique individuals, and promote their development in all areas.

Because of this individuality, it is impossible to develop a schedule in the traditional sense. Children will get to all of the above events, but in their own order at their own time. No two schedules will ever be exactly alike.

To provide you with insight on what you should be observing, below is a sample full-day schedule for five-month-old DeShawn during one day (Dodge, Rudick, and Berke 2011). The schedule focuses on DeShawn and his interactions with his teacher Samanda. While only DeShawn is featured in this schedule, it should be remembered that Samanda is also the primary teacher for other children in the program.

As you review DeShawn's schedule, bear in mind that as infants mature, their schedules will change to reflect their increasing growth and developing skills. For example, mobile infants will be more social and able to do many more things than DeShawn can at his stage of development.

DeShawn, 5 months—12/16

| Morning | Afternoon |

Teacher planning time: All the teachers in DeShawn's room meet as a group before any children arrive to discuss the children they care for. They make sure all necessary supplies are at hand and the room is set up as needed. They do daily health and safety checks and wash their hands in preparation for the children's arrival.

Arrival: DeShawn's mom drops him off with his primary teacher, Samanda. She tells Samanda that DeShawn is hungry.

Eating: Samanda gets a bottle, already prepared by his mom, and rocks DeShawn in a rocking chair, talking to him as she feeds and burps him.

Diapering: Samanda carries DeShawn to the diapering table, secures him with the safety belt, and changes him. She talks with him about what she is doing and the things she has planned for their day together. DeShawn coos and gurgles.

Naptime: Samanda offers DeShawn a toy to play with, but he starts to close his eyes. She puts him in his crib (on his back) and rubs his belly as he falls asleep.

Diapering: DeShawn wakes up, and Samanda greets him and removes him from the crib. She carries him to the changing table to check his diaper. Though it is barely wet, she decides to put on a fresh diaper.

Indoor play: Samanda seats DeShawn on a mat and offers a sensory rattle ball for him to play with. As he shakes and mouths the ball, Samanda talks with DeShawn about what he is doing and how his actions make the ball react.

Eating: Hearing DeShawn give out a short, low-pitched cry and observing him suck his fist, Samanda decides that DeShawn is hungry. She offers him a bottle, and he drinks half of it.

Diapering/dressing: Samanda sings to DeShawn as she changes his soiled diaper on the changing table. She dresses him to go outside, narrating her actions as she does them.

Outdoor play: Samanda places DeShawn on a mat with some leaves that the two of them picked up off the ground. DeShawn explores the leaves with all of his senses, delighting in the way they crinkle when he holds them.

Diapering/dressing: Samanda and DeShawn go back indoors. She takes off his jacket and secures him to the changing table, where she changes his diaper. While doing so, she discusses all of the things that DeShawn did with the leaf.

Eating: DeShawn and Samanda sit on a glider while Samanda gives him a bottle. She sings to him while he nestles in her lap. DeShawn falls asleep before his bottle is finished.

Naptime: Samanda carries DeShawn to his crib, places him on his back, and he quickly falls back asleep.

Diapering/dressing: While changing DeShawn's diaper, Samanda asks him questions like "Who's the happiest baby?" and "Who makes me happy every day?" and then plays a game of peekaboo with him.

Indoor play: Samanda sits on the floor with DeShawn and Michael and reads the boys a board book, pointing out objects and animals as she reads. DeShawn occasionally grabs the book from her and mouths it while Michael flails his hands.

Departure: Samanda spots DeShawn's mother picking up papers in the greeting area and getting DeShawn's jacket. Samanda beckons her to join them. She hands DeShawn to his mother. They talk for five minutes or so, going over DeShawn's day. Samanda then waves good-bye.

Debriefing: Samanda meets with her colleagues to review the day and make plans for the future. She discusses the skills she is targeting for DeShawn and gets input from her colleagues.

What Program Structure Should Look Like

In a high-quality program, the program structure supports and enhances children's growth, development, and learning. In the chart below, you will find examples of an appropriate program structure and how it supports infants' progress.

What you should see	Why
Teachers and infants follow a flexible schedule of simple and consistent routines that are tailored to meet the needs of individual children.	Each infant has an individual schedule for sleeping, diapering, and feeding. When their needs are met promptly and consistently, infants develop a sense of trust that they are secure and cared for. Infant teachers must adjust to each infant's unique schedule, rather than expecting all of the infants to follow the same schedule.
Activities are scheduled between routines.	While routines like eating, sleeping, and diapering take up a major part of an infant's day, it's important to schedule time for engaging with children and doing varied activities like playing with toys and listening to a book being read. Learning experiences such as these support development in all domains.
Teachers take cues from infants as to when a routine or activity should begin and when it should end.	Through ongoing observation and partnering with families, teachers will learn how each child signals the need for food, a diaper change, or play. They can then respond with the kind of care and attention that is familiar and effective for the individual child. Children create the infant schedule. If a child no longer wants a bottle or has woken up from a nap, then that activity is over and it's time to move on to the next.
Teachers take advantage of "teachable moments."	Individualized schedules for infants need to be flexible, not just to bodily needs but to events too. Infants benefit from unplanned learning experiences. For example, if a sudden snow flurry begins during outdoor time, teachers can delay going back indoors to allow infants to feel the wet snow on their faces and reach out for snowflakes.
Family members and teachers take time to exchange information about an infant's day or evening, progress in gaining skills, and just to touch base.	Being separated from their babies is clearly hard on family members who are eager to know how their infant is faring during the day. Families need daily reassurance that things are going well. In addition, by exchanging information, all adults can provide consistency and security at the program and at home.
Teachers take infants outside daily.	Being outside offers children different kinds of sensory experiences in nature and different things to explore. To ensure comfort, both adults and children should be dressed for the weather. Being outdoors refreshes and energizes both infants and their teachers.

What you should see	Why
Infants play with one or two other children during the day.	Children are naturally drawn to others. By spending time with other children, they develop social skills and learn to enjoy and relate to others.
Teachers talk to and interact with infants in a relaxed manner during repeated routines, such as feeding, diapering, and dressing.	Routines are opportunities for teaching, learning, and building relationships. By hearing their teacher's familiar voice, young infants learn about language and feel safe in the teacher's care. Mobile infants learn new concepts, such as the names of facial features and how cause and effect works. Children also get the message that their teachers value these one-on-one times and don't regard routines as chores to hurry through.
Mobile infants actively participate in routines, doing as much as they can for themselves.	Although it slows down the schedule, engaging mobile infants in routines teaches them important self-help skills and promotes independence. For example, a child can hold the diaper until the teacher is ready for it and help wash and dry her own hands before being lifted off the table. An older child can pull off her socks or lift her arms when changing a shirt.
Teachers take infants out of their cribs as soon as they notice the child is awake.	Spending a little time gazing at hands or looking around the room is a fine activity for a few minutes. However, leaving a child awake and waiting in a crib—even if the child doesn't complain—can mean the child is not being stimulated by taking part in a routine or activity.
Mobile infants eat lunch together at child-size tables with two to three other children.	Mobile infants no longer need to be fed on demand the way that young infants do. As children grow and learn to feed themselves, with and without utensils, they enjoy the company of others while they dine.
Teachers invite mobile infants to get out of their chairs after eating and move on to another activity.	Sitting at the table can be confining, and children should not be forced to remain seated. Mobile infants need to be free to move safely and explore and learn from their environment.

When you observe the twelve items noted above in place, it is likely that your program's schedule is serving infants well. Use the checklist in appendix B to observe how well your program meets these criteria. For items that your program is not yet addressing well, work with teachers to devise and implement an action plan for improvement. As a supervisor, you are responsible for ensuring that the program structure optimally supports children's growth, development, and learning.

When the Program Structure Needs Further Adjusting

For deeper insight into the effectiveness of your program's structure, it's important to observe children and teachers throughout the entire day. It's one thing to have a well-thought-out schedule on paper. However, unless the schedule allows children the time they need to be involved in routines and activities and to transition smoothly from one activity to the next, it is of little use. If you spot children and teachers engaged in behaviors such as those described below, the program structure may need adjusting. Discuss with teachers the warning sign, reasons why the behavior might be happening, and the possible solutions noted in the third column. Help them implement these countermeasures or others they develop to make your program's structure more effective.

Note: Some of the warning signs listed below may be caused by factors other than the program's structure or by a combination of the program's structure and other factors. Regular observations will provide information about the precise cause of the problem.

Warning sign	Why this might be happening	How educators can address the problem
All of the children in the room are fed, diapered, and take naps at the same time, according to an established schedule.	Teachers believe that children should follow a standard schedule to make sure that everyone's needs are met.	Hold a workshop on using a primary caregiving approach. Underscore the need to meet infants' needs according to individual time clocks—not a preset schedule. Discuss how primary caregiving allows teachers to meet children's needs promptly and consistently.
Individual children do the same things every day, without variation.	Teachers don't know how to balance infants' needs for consistency with their needs for challenging and stimulating new experiences.	Discuss your observations with teachers. Review which parts of the schedule and which activities should remain consistent. Offer suggestions about when and how to introduce new activities.
Teachers rush through routines, quickly returning children to play activities.	Teachers believe that children only learn through play and want to maximize children's learning opportunities.	Using one routine as an example, ask teachers to list all of the things a child might learn through the experience. Suggest they make posters to remind them of what they can say and do with infants during routines. Brainstorm together ways that teachers can introduce and reinforce concepts and build relationships while feeding, diapering, and dressing children.
Mobile infants sit at child-size tables by themselves eating lunch.	Teachers are trying to keep the children's schedules 100 percent individualized and feed each child when they believe she is hungry. They allow mealtimes to go on as long as needed for everyone to eat.	Remind teachers that from about eleven months on, mobile infants can sit comfortably at a low table and feed themselves. This makes eating meals a social experience. Suggest having mobile infants eat meals in groups of two or three at a set time. Make this a pleasant event where children can participate and enjoy being part of a community.

Warning sign	Why this might be happening	How educators can address the problem
All activities are led by teachers.	Teachers think they must provide direct instruction to ensure children learn new skills, concepts, and knowledge.	Reassure teachers that children learn by exploring toys and materials and the environment. Using all of their senses, they see for themselves how their world works. Model how to let children take the lead in an activity with the adult interacting and offering support.
Children sit in cribs or infant seats for long periods of time, looking uninvolved and passive.	Teachers may be overwhelmed by caring for more than one child at a time. They may confine children so they can meet the needs of others. Sometimes families arrive with a sleeping infant in a car seat. Rather than wake the child, the teacher lets the child continue sleeping, not realizing that this is a dangerous practice. (Infants can maneuver themselves into positions that can lead to suffocation.)	Plan opportunities—such as a visit to another classroom or program—where teachers can learn from others who found ways to care for several children at one time. Or observe teachers and hold coaching sessions to offer strength-based feedback focused on what they do well. Then jointly discuss ways to solve problems such as this one.
Teachers take turns carrying out a specific routine or activity. For example, one teacher diapers all of the children all of the time while another sits on the floor playing with children as soon as they are diapered.	Teachers might prefer one routine over another. Or teachers think it's good for children to get to know multiple teachers closely. Or an assistant or less experienced teacher is assigned this task because it is thought to require fewer skills.	Discuss with teachers why a primary caregiving approach helps children bond and develop a sense of trust and helps teachers get to know individual infants and the best ways to meet their needs. Explain why an assembly-line approach to routines means that children don't build relationships with the adults caring for them. And, as routines are important learning times, they require the same skills as any other activity.
Family members are rushed out of the room upon arrival in the morning.	Teachers believe that children suffer less separation anxiety if family members leave immediately. They may not value parental input on how best to care for a child and see no need to exchange information.	Help teachers understand that infants and family members need time to separate in a way that is comfortable for them, and that the daily schedule should accommodate this need. Review the benefits of engaging families as partners for the adults, but most importantly for the children.

Curriculum: Activities and Experiences

An early childhood curriculum is a written framework that guides teaching and learning. Like the title of this book, it provides the what, why, and how of implementing a high-quality learning program for young children. Infant curricula are based on relationships, focus on routines as opportunities for learning, and reflect early learning standards for this age group.

Foundations Underlying Quality

Before observing teachers implementing the curriculum with infants, you will need to be sure your program has a high-quality curriculum in place. Because infant programs have differing goals and missions, there is no one curriculum that every infant program should use. Some programs design their own curriculum to meet specific needs and circumstances. Others select and purchase a published curriculum, such as Teaching Strategies' *The Creative Curriculum for Infants, Toddlers & Twos* or *The HighScope Infant-Toddler Curriculum,* both of which are research-based and validated.

Whether designing your own curriculum or adopting a commercial one, a high-quality infant curriculum should meet these criteria:

☀ It is consistent with your program's goals and objectives.

☀ It is aligned with mandated standards, be they federal (in the case of Early Head Start and military child development programs), state, local, or tribal agency.

☀ It supports all areas of children's development: emotional, social, physical, language, and cognitive.

☀ There is documented evidence of the curriculum's success in fostering children's development.

☀ It is relationship-based; it emphasizes the importance of building relationships among children, teachers, and families.

☀ It emphasizes using routines as opportunities to teach and learn.

☀ It describes how to set up the environment to ensure health, safety, and movement, and it allows for choice.

☀ The roles and expectations for teachers are described in depth.

☀ Children have many opportunities to explore the world and experiment through play.

☀ Learning activities and experiences allow children to play alone and near others.

☀ Teaching strategies are differentiated, based on individual skills, abilities, temperaments, interests, learning preferences, home languages, family structures, and cultures.

☀ It can be tailored to support children with specific disabilities.

☀ Teachers and families are considered partners in their children's learning at the program and at home.

☀ Observation-based assessment is used to document children's developmental progress.

A high-quality infant curriculum guides teachers, administrators, and families as they work together to support and maximize children's development and learning.

What the Curriculum Should Look Like

In a high-quality program, the curriculum is implemented as it was designed to be used. Teachers may make adaptations to fit the makeup of their program, but they adhere to the curriculum's stated goals, objectives, and mission. In the chart below, you will find examples of what the routines and experiences in a high-quality infant curriculum would look like and why.

What you should see	Why
Teachers promptly respond when infants communicate through verbal and nonverbal cues that they are tired, are hungry, or need a clean and dry diaper.	By recognizing children's cues and responding to their needs promptly and cheerfully, teachers make children feel safe and secure—and free to learn. Through nurturing relationships, children learn to co-regulate their emotions and eventually to self-regulate. This is a hallmark of early childhood development.
Teachers introduce and reinforce skills based on what they observe children doing and learning.	When teachers observe children, reflect on what the children are experiencing, and then provide support and materials, they are facilitating each child's growth, development, and learning. The experiences teachers plan for individual children reflect the child's current stage of development.
Teachers use routines as opportunities to promote learning.	Much of an infant's day is devoted to routines like eating, dressing, napping, and diapering. Teachers can capitalize on these experiences as opportunities for learning. For example, bottle feedings are times to talk and form close attachments.
Children play with materials that they have selected for themselves; they might mouth a book or shake a rattle.	When children choose an activity, they are naturally motivated to learn. After observing, teachers can extend learning by narrating the baby's actions and offering suggestions: "You squeezed the duck. What did you hear? It made a loud noise. Try squeezing it again."

What you should see	**Why**
Teachers regularly observe children's interactions and activities, document what they see and hear, and maintain individual portfolios. Teachers steer children to activities that are a good fit for their observed developmental levels and interests.	Observation is a key way to collect the information needed to plan an individualized infant curriculum that allows a child to practice, master, and gain new skills. Observations can also support accountability and demonstrate success in addressing early learning standards.
Children use their large muscles in various activities throughout the day, such as batting at a mobile with their feet, rolling over, crawling, pulling themselves up, walking, and rolling a ball.	Gross-motor development is a major focus of learning for infants. Teachers should engage infants in activities both indoors and outdoors that will help them develop and master new movement skills.
Children use the small muscles in their hands in various activities throughout the day, such as holding a bottle, turning the pages of a board book, putting large wooden beads in a container, or building a three-block tower.	Fine-motor development is another major focus for infants. Teachers should provide materials, experiences, and encouragement to use, develop, and strengthen small muscles.
Teachers engage both verbal and nonverbal infants in conversation during the day's routines and activities.	The development of language and literacy skills is one of the hallmarks of the early childhood years. By conversing with infants even before they know how to speak, teachers help to wire the children's brains for language.
Children solve problems (nest cups inside each other), explore cause and effect (turn the handle on a jack-in-the-box), and apply old knowledge to new situations (shake a tambourine like a rattle to make noise) throughout the day.	Infants can build their thinking skills during routines, transitions, play, and activities. Teachers facilitate cognitive development by providing open-ended materials and interacting with children by narrating the child's actions and results, asking questions, and making suggestions.
Children express themselves through the creative arts. For example, infants might coo while listening to a lullaby, pretend to move like a dog, or paint the sidewalk with water.	The arts are a gateway for learning. For example, children learn about language and communicating by responding to music orally and through movement. The visual arts enable children to experiment with materials and express their feelings as they pound dough and fill a paper with color.

What you should see	Why
Teachers ensure that the curriculum is accessible to all children, including those with special needs. For example, a child having separation anxiety looks at pictures of his family and listens to a recording of his mother singing a lullaby at naptime, a child with a hospitalized parent receives extra attention and comfort, and a child with orthopedic impairments uses adapted eating utensils.	Every child has unique strengths and challenges. A high-quality curriculum encourages teachers to modify activities, interactions, and materials as needed to allow all children to fully participate and benefit from the program. This does not mean that each child needs his own curriculum. Rather, it means that the same curriculum needs to be made accessible for each child.
Family members share their skills and interests and play with, read to, and otherwise engage the children. For example, a grandparent sits in a rocking chair reading a book to his grandchild and her friend, a mother nurses her baby on a lunch break, or a parent rolls a ball back and forth with a few children.	Research show that when families partner with early childhood programs, children learn more and feel more competent and confident. It is important that family members feel welcomed by the program and are encouraged to volunteer during the day when children can see them and their teachers working together.

When you observe the twelve items noted above in place, it is likely that your program's curriculum is serving infants well. Use the checklist in appendix B to observe how well your program meets these criteria. For items that your program is not yet addressing well, work with teachers to devise and implement an action plan for improvement. As a supervisor, you are responsible for ensuring that the curriculum optimally supports children's growth, development, and learning.

When the Curriculum Needs Further Adjusting

For deeper insight into the effectiveness of your program's curriculum, it's important to observe children and teachers at various times throughout the day. To be fully effective, a high-quality curriculum should be implemented as designed, with fidelity. For example, if teachers were to exclude infants younger than six months from using the chosen curriculum, believing they are too young to participate in a formal curriculum, this would be a misinterpretation of how the curriculum is intended to be used.

If you spot children and teachers engaged in behaviors such as those described below, the curriculum's implementation may need adjusting. Discuss with teachers the warning sign, reasons why the behavior might be happening, and the possible solutions noted in the third column. Help them implement these countermeasures or others they develop to increase the effectiveness of curriculum implementation.

Note: Some of the warning signs listed below may be caused by factors other than implementation problems or by a combination of implementation problems and other factors. Regular observations will provide information about the precise cause of the problem.

Warning sign	Why this might be happening	How educators can address the problem
Teachers tend to the needs of young infants but ignore mobile infants' requests for attention.	Teachers believe that young infants need their full-time focus and older children can "entertain" themselves.	Meet with teachers to discuss the needs of mobile infants. Emphasize that even though mobile infants can at times occupy themselves, they need teachers' attention just as much as younger babies do. Strategize ways to interact with young infants and mobile infants at the same time. Later observe teachers and decide together if further training is needed.
Teachers focus on helping children develop cognitive and language skills, minimizing time on social and emotional skill development.	Teachers think that increasing children's academic skills are the most important part of their role and that children will learn social and emotional skills at home with their families.	Hold a workshop on infant development. Highlight infant development in all domains, noting that learning is integrated during the early years. Emphasize the importance of social and emotional development in fostering a sense of trust, which is a foundation for learning.
Teachers remove infants from activities they are enjoying to participate in activities teachers have planned.	Teachers are eager to introduce children to activities they have planned; they think that their planned activities will better engage the children.	Remind teachers of the importance of respecting children's needs and interests. Make sure that everyone agrees that following children's cues is the best way to support their development.
Young infants all do the same activity at the same time, such as taking two-hour naps at the same time every afternoon.	Teachers think the easiest approach to caregiving is to have all of the children eat and nap at the same time. Or teachers believe the only way they can take a break is to have children go to sleep at the same time.	Hold a workshop on the philosophy of the curriculum. Underscore the basic tenet that adults respond to children's needs on demand. This creates a sense of security and trust that allows children to feel safe enough to experiment and try new things. Teachers need to be responsive to children, not do what's easiest.
Teachers direct and lead all of the children's activities.	Teachers think that children learn best when they impart knowledge and show the children what to do.	Review with teachers that in an infant curriculum, teachers should facilitate learning by allowing children to choose what they want to explore and how. While it's sometimes appropriate to plan and lead a flexible activity, teachers need to allow children to do things on their own. With the teachers' permission, video record them interacting with children, and together discuss how they do and do not pick up on children's cues. At a later time, again video record the teachers to highlight their successes in picking up children's cues.

Warning sign	Why this might be happening	How educators can address the problem
Teachers leave children to play with toys while they sit at a table and plan.	Teachers think that once children are occupied and busy, they can use that time to carry out other responsibilities. Perhaps teachers do not have a dedicated time for planning.	Visit the classroom to model how to interact with children playing with toys. Afterward discuss all of the learning opportunities that would have been missed had there been no adult there to interact with the children and guide their focus. Review the work schedule to make sure teachers have sufficient planning time.
Only mobile infants do activities such as art, music, water play, and dramatic play.	Teachers believe that young infants will not get anything out of these experiences.	Hold a professional development session on how to engage young infants in activities. For example, young infants can crumple fabrics and papers to gain a sensory foundation for art. For music experiences, young infants respond to different types of music, sounds, and singing. Young infants enjoy splashing and playing with rubber toys in a basin with about an inch of water. Babies can also play with dolls and stuffed animals and imitate their teachers' expressions and actions.
Teachers show children how to use materials the "right way."	Teachers believe they are helping children learn. Also, they want children to experience success.	Meet with teachers to discuss why creativity can blossom only when children are free to make mistakes and that innovation occurs when people think "outside the box"—ignoring the "right" way. Give children open-ended toys to play with, and together observe how children's experimentations help them learn how to solve problems and think creatively.

Supportive Interactions

In a high-quality infant room, the teachers ensure health and safety, and they spend plenty of time getting to know and respond to each baby in their care. Each teacher is assigned to be the primary caregiver of a small group of babies. Other teachers assist as needed, but one teacher becomes the "expert" in caring for and supporting the assigned babies. The primary caregiver is the main point of contact for the family, typically exchanging information and sharing the joy in the baby's accomplishments every day.

Foundations Underlying Quality

How might a visitor to an infant classroom recognize the kinds of interactions that support infants' growth, development, and learning? What are the signs that each baby receives individualized care? Teachers' supportive interactions with infants share the following characteristics:

* Interactions take place at an infant's eye level and where infants spend their time. For example, teachers coo and babble with babies at the diapering table, sit down on the ground or floor to help babies interpret what they see and hear in the world, talk with babies during bottle feedings, and narrate what they are doing while kneeling to help a mobile infant put on her shoes to go outdoors.

* Teachers reflect and incorporate information provided by families. Teachers might refer to children's families in conversation: "Your daddy said you tried bananas on Saturday and think they are delicious." Or they might implement caregiving strategies suggested by families: "Your mom says that you like to sit up now. Let's see how you do."

* Teachers communicate using facial expressions, touch, and words. Infants watch, listen, and learn all the time from the important people in their lives. From an early age, they recognize and respond to emotions—both positive and negative. They probably don't know the cause of certain feelings, but they do know when someone is happy to see them or annoyed by something they did or didn't do.

* Teachers use active watching and listening to read and respond to babies' cues. In addition to various kinds of crying, infants ask for what they need through individual cues. One baby might arch her back when she wants to get down on the carpet. Another might wriggle in a teacher's arms. A baby might stare at an object she wants. An attentive teacher will notice the stare and figure out what the child is requesting.

But most of all, supportive interactions tell infants, "I like being with you. I notice what you are doing and applaud your progress. You are an important person in your family and in our classroom."

What Supportive Interactions Should Look Like

Because teachers are the most important component of an infant program, their interactions with infants are crucial to providing high-quality care. Infants learn basic trust as they develop warm, secure, reciprocal relationships with the important adults in their lives—usually family members and teachers. This sense of trust encourages infants to explore, learn, and gain new skills. Look for the following kinds of interactions when you visit an infant room.

What you should see	Why
Teachers sit on the floor with infants reading books, singing songs, talking, playing with toys, and so on.	Teachers are most effective in building relationships with infants when they are on the child's level. This position allows teachers to be both physically and emotionally close to children.
Teachers comfort a child who is frightened when a new person enters the room.	As infants learn more about their world and the people in it, they distinguish people who are familiar from those who are not. At nine to twelve months and again at seventeen to eighteen months, an infant may become anxious around strangers. This is a normal part of development. With a teacher's help, an infant can get used to the new person.
Teachers show pleasure and encouragement when a child attempts and achieves a goal.	Throughout infancy, babies are rapidly gaining new skills. They work hard to learn to sit, crawl, stand, and walk. When adults acknowledge their efforts and accomplishments, infants are eager to continue gaining new skills.
Teachers respond to infants' communication, whether in the form of cries, gestures, coos, gurgles, or first words, by interpreting the communication and talking back to the child.	When teachers respond, infants learn about the give-and-take of conversations and that it is enjoyable to share feelings and ideas with others. This kind of encouragement leads infants to continue trying to express themselves through language.
Teachers encourage mobile infants' use of self-help skills as soon as they are developmentally ready to do so.	Mobile infants are building a sense of competence—recognizing what they can do. They are eager to perform many tasks for themselves and proudly learn to hang coats on hooks, remove clothing, feed themselves, wash hands, wipe a table, and more.
Teachers accept spills and messes as a natural part of learning as mobile infants practice feeding themselves and take part in activities such as art and sand and water play.	Some explorations and experiments are tidy, but most result in messes and spills. It's best for teachers to adopt a matter-of-fact attitude to cleaning up. The goal is to stay calm so the child is not discouraged from further explorations.
Teachers give attention to several infants at the same time.	An infant room is a learning community in which children learn to share their teachers with each other. A teacher might hold a young infant after a feeding while rolling a ball to two mobile infants and telling another child, "I'll read to you in just a minute."
Teachers model pretend behaviors and join in children's pretend play.	One of the ways children learn to make sense of the world is through dramatic play. A teacher can show a child how to pretend to talk on the phone or feed a bottle to a stuffed animal. Imitating adult activities helps infants express their feelings and understand the world around them.

What you should see	Why
Teachers use information shared by a child's family when talking with the child.	When teachers incorporate information shared by families in conversations, infants learn that the important people in their lives all care about them, making them feel more secure.
Teachers vary their tone of voice, nonverbal responses, and interactions with infants to fit the child's temperament, whether flexible, active, or cautious.	An infant's temperament is fixed at birth but affected by nature and nurture. All temperaments are equally worthy and appropriate. When teachers get to know how a child typically reacts and relates to the world, they can tailor their interactions accordingly. They accept who the child is and do not expect the child to suddenly be different.
Teachers learn and use a few important words and phrases in the child's home language.	Children tend to associate their home language with family and a nurturing atmosphere. Using the home language at the program promotes a sense of comfort and safety and sends children the message that they are valued for who they are.
Mobile infants begin to play alongside each other and show signs of beginning empathy.	Children learn from watching the adults who care for them. They copy the behaviors they have seen and try them out on their own. Children who attend child development programs get to know their classmates well and develop strong feelings for them.

When the twelve items noted above are in place, the interactions in your program are likely to support infants' growth, development, and learning. Use the checklist in appendix B to observe how well your program meets these criteria. For items that your program is not yet addressing well, work with teachers to devise and implement an action plan for improvement. As a supervisor, you are responsible for ensuring that all teachers' supportive interactions are optimally serving children and teachers.

When Interactions Need Further Adjusting

For deeper insight into the effectiveness of the supportive interactions between teachers and infants, it's important to observe in the classroom. If you spot warning signs such as those in the examples described below, it's time to look more closely and try to identify what might be causing the situation. Discuss the possible solutions noted in the third column with teachers and help them better understand how supportive interactions nurture and foster the development of infants.

Note: Some of the warning signs listed below may be caused by factors other than nonsupportive interactions or by a combination of nonsupportive interactions and other factors. Regular observations will provide information about the precise cause of the problem.

Warning sign	Why this might be happening	How educators can address the problem
Teachers seldom talk to and with infants; they carry out routines in silence and rarely communicate with babies.	Teachers may feel embarrassed about talking, singing, and playing with infants. Perhaps they don't realize that these relationship-building activities give babies a foundation for learning and using language.	Visit the classroom and model interacting with infants. Ask someone to video record what you say and do and how the babies respond. Use the video to demonstrate how coos and gurgles are the beginning of communication and learning the give-and-take of conversation.
Teachers take primary caregiving to an extreme, rarely interacting with babies who are assigned to another teacher.	Teachers may not know each other well and spend little time communicating about the babies in each other's care. They may not know how to address the needs of babies other than the ones for whom they provide primary caregiving. Teachers may not want to share the baby with anyone else, thinking they won't know how to care for the child or that they are interfering with another teacher's responsibilities.	Commend teachers for their primary caregiving skills, while clarifying the definition of primary caregiving. Plan to include more opportunities to share information about each child in the group during teachers meetings. Encourage teachers to get to know all the children in the group and learn what are the most effective ways to meet each child's needs.
Teachers ignore infants' requests for engagement, assistance, or to have a need met.	Teachers may think, "I'm busy and will get to him when I'm done." They may not realize that just saying, "I hear you and will be there soon," lets babies know their requests were received and helps them wait for attention.	Lead a role play or guided imagery in which teachers reflect on what it feels like to make a request and then be ignored. Discuss how babies might feel in similar situations. Explain that recognition can be verbal or combined with a simple touch until the teacher is able to focus on the baby.
Teachers do not greet and exchange information with families and infants at drop-off and pickup times.	Teachers may be uncomfortable talking with families or may not understand what everyone gains from strong and equal teacher-family relationships. They may view families' questions and concerns as criticism of the care their child receives.	Acknowledge that it is difficult to switch from the skills used to support infants to the skills used to interact with adults. Offer practical tips for making this switch. Explain that when teachers and families exchange information about a child's day, all adults will feel like partners and children will see that the important people in their life can be trusted.

Warning sign	Why this might be happening	How educators can address the problem
Teachers leave at break time or at the end of their shift without notifying colleagues.	Teachers may think everyone knows their schedule and see no need to say good-bye.	To address this behavior, have a one-on-one conversation to focus on two points: 1. It is not safe to leave without handing off caregiving responsibilities to a colleague. Someone needs to know that the teacher is no longer looking out for his or her assigned children. 2. Leaving without notifying colleagues is discourteous and disrespectful. Invite the teacher to suggest a plan for letting colleagues know of his or her departure.
Teachers offer toys and other interesting materials but do not actually play with infants.	Teachers may be busy carrying out routines and not realize that playing with infants is an important way to support development and learning in all domains. They may think that infants can just explore on their own and don't need adult assistance to play.	Review the environment to make sure all items needed for routines are easy to reach so diapering and feeding go smoothly. This gives teachers time to interact with children rather than looking for supplies. Next, model how to play with infants and point out what infants are learning through adult participation. For example, "Playing peekaboo with Justin isn't just fun. He is learning about object permanence—his teddy is still under the blanket even if he can't see it."
Teachers rarely talk with one another.	Teachers may not know each other well because there was no time for an orientation when they started work or because they have little time for planning. Perhaps teachers meetings offer little time for sharing and interacting with colleagues.	Meet with teachers with the explicit purpose of helping them get to know each other better. Review the program's planning and orientation process. Interview teachers for a program-wide newsletter, and create bulletin boards that introduce teachers to families and to each other.
Teachers seldom talk with preverbal babies and say little to babies during daily routines and activities.	Teachers may not realize how much babies learn from their verbal and nonverbal interactions. They may think there is no need to talk to a baby who can't understand or respond to words.	Visit the classroom and model supportive interactions with babies during routines. Invite teachers to video record you, and then include the video as part of a workshop on supportive interactions. Be sure to make a few "mistakes," so teachers can point them out and discuss what would have been a more appropriate response to a baby's cue.

Positive Guidance

In a high-quality infant program, the teachers support development and learning, including learning what behaviors are acceptable and how to manage and express strong feelings. Through positive guidance, teachers acknowledge and accept an infant's emotions, whatever they may be. The infants learn that it is okay to feel angry or frustrated, and that teachers can be trusted to meet their needs as soon as they are available to do so. Teachers help infants gradually learn that they can express their feelings through crying, but also through gazing, pointing, cooing, smiling, and eventually through language.

Self-regulation, as defined in the introduction and used throughout this book, is the ability to control bodily functions, manage powerful emotions, and maintain focus and attention. It is frequently regarded as an important goal during the early childhood years. The development of self-regulation begins in infancy. By the time children enter elementary school, they have mastered toileting and eating and many other self-help skills. They can recognize, name, and manage their strong feelings. They can delay gratification and wait for a turn or the teacher's attention, complete assigned tasks, and figure out ways to get along with each other in a classroom community. Through positive guidance from infancy on, they have learned to behave in acceptable ways and can use language to make requests and share ideas and feelings.

At first, adults play a major role in facilitating and supporting the child. "The adults put a young baby's pacifier back in her mouth, provide a soft blanket for a toddler falling asleep, and use consistent routines to support self-regulation by helping very young children know what to expect" (Gillespie and Seibel 2006). Soon children gain other skills that allow them to self-soothe, feed themselves, make choices, return toys to the shelves, and enjoy being with their teachers and peers.

Foundations Underlying Quality

How might a visitor to an infant classroom recognize the use of positive guidance strategies that support infants' self-regulation? What are the signs that teachers acknowledge and respond to infants' emotions while helping them learn acceptable ways to make requests and express ideas? Positive guidance for infants reflects the following beliefs and actions:

☀ Babies and their behaviors are neither good nor bad. They are busy using all of their senses to understand their world and have their basic needs met.

☀ Babies don't cry or behave in certain ways to annoy the adults in their lives. For example, they do not have the cognitive skills needed to plan and carry out particular actions just to be irksome.

☀ Babies respond to positive guidance. Teachers can use positive guidance strategies to point out potential dangers and redirect children to safe and enjoyable activities.

☀ Babies are learning all the time as they use their senses to explore the people and things in their environment. They watch and listen to adults and mimic their behavior.

What Positive Guidance Should Look Like

In an infant program, teachers use a variety of individualized positive guidance strategies to prevent behaviors that are unsafe and encourage behaviors that support learning and development. Teachers use soft voices that help babies feel safe and secure. In the following examples, you will see what strategies and outcomes should be in place when you visit an infant program and why these are important.

What you should see	Why
A safe, well-planned, developmentally appropriate environment that supports teachers, families, and all the infants in the group.	Creating an environment that reflects infants' current stages of development, cultures, home languages, families, abilities, and interests will prevent most problem behaviors that are a result of adults' inappropriate expectations for the group.
Teachers respond consistently and promptly to infants who are crying; teachers hold and cuddle infants who seem inconsolable until they have calmed.	Infants learn to trust when their needs are met in response to their cries. This is a first step on the way to self-regulation. Babies cry for many reasons, even when all their physical needs have been met. Often they just need more time to calm themselves.
Teachers hold young infants close, look into their faces, smile, and talk with them; the infants respond with coos and gurgles.	Young infants are learning to recognize the important people in their lives. Close physical contact helps infants develop attachments with these adults, which in turn contributes to a sense of security and a willingness to learn positive behaviors.
Teachers redirect babies from potentially frustrating or dangerous situations, such as pulling something off a counter or trying to climb out of a crib, by physically moving them or offering an interesting play material.	Redirection is a positive guidance strategy that works in most situations. It helps babies learn about limits and what they can or cannot do.
Teachers wait to see whether infants can solve problems on their own before stepping in to help.	Infants are a long way from complete independence, but problem solving is an important skill to nurture even in the earliest years. An infant might retrieve a ball by crawling to reach it. Older children use problem-solving skills to resolve disagreements and figure out ways to play with others.
Teachers offer interesting alternatives when two children want to play with the same toy.	Infants are not ready to share, but most times infants will be happy with the alternative and won't notice that their first choice has been replaced with something equally interesting, if a duplicate toy is not available.
Teachers model caring behaviors, such as stroking another baby's hair instead of pulling it.	Infants are very interested in exploring their world—including the other babies in their group. They do not realize that they are hurting someone by pulling hair. When teachers model appropriate ways to touch, the babies will imitate the adults' behaviors.

What you should see	Why
Teachers say no only when it is absolutely necessary to keep a child safe.	Saving no for extreme situations teaches children that this is an important request. When infants hear no too often, they no longer pay attention to it.
Teachers frequently offer choices to older infants and then accept children's decisions.	Children need a lot of practice to learn how to make good decisions, and teachers can provide opportunities to choose, for example, which shirt to put on when their clothing needs to be changed or which toy to play with. Making decisions is a part of becoming independent and developing self-regulation.
Teachers acknowledge infants' communications and activities through verbal and nonverbal responses and by frequently using their names.	Infants are developing a sense of who they are; using their name helps them understand that they are unique individuals. Teachers' interactions demonstrate respect for what each child says and does.
Teachers invite mobile infants to help do real jobs, such as helping to clear dishes, clean up toys, and mop up a spill.	Infants learn prosocial behaviors, such as being helpful, when teachers provide opportunities for children to participate. These activities are fun for infants and help build a sense of competence. When infants do things that adults do, they tend to feel positive about their abilities.
Teachers demonstrate respect for children's families and cultures.	Teachers and families are partners in nurturing a child's growth, development, and learning. Babies feel most comfortable when their home and program experiences and setting are as consistent as possible.

When the twelve items noted above are in place, the program's positive guidance approach is likely to support infants' growth, development, and learning and help them begin to gain self-regulation skills. As a supervisor, you are responsible for ensuring that teachers use positive guidance to help children learn how to use acceptable behaviors.

When Guidance Strategies Need Further Adjusting

For deeper insight into the effectiveness of the program's positive guidance approach, it's important to observe the interactions and activities of infants and their teachers. Knowledge of positive guidance strategies does not always translate into their effective use. If you spot warning signs such as those in the examples described below, it's time to look more closely and try to identify what might be causing the situation. Discuss the possible solutions noted in the third column with teachers and help them better understand how the use of positive guidance is a teaching strategy that helps children learn how to behave in acceptable ways.

Note: Some of the warning signs listed below may be caused by factors other than inappropriate guidance strategies or by a combination of inappropriate guidance strategies and other factors. Regular observations will provide information about the precise cause of the problem.

Warning sign	Why this might be happening	How educators can address the problem
Teachers make negative comments and facial expressions while at work; as a result, infants do not engage with them and families and colleagues avoid interactions with them.	Teachers may not realize that they are sharing their unhappy feelings with others—including the infants in their care. They may not have the skills needed to enjoy their work or do not place enough value on nurturing infants as a profession.	Hold a private coaching session with the teacher. Discuss the program's philosophy and overall approach and commitment to families and children. Point out the teacher's strengths and ask about his or her own professional goals. Offer professional development if you think this will help to build on the individual's strengths. In some cases, it may be most appropriate to counsel the individual to choose another profession.
Teachers rush through routines such as diapering and feeding, spending little one-on-one time building relationships with babies.	Teachers may view routines as chores to be completed as soon as possible. They may not see them as opportunities for babies to learn and build the kinds of trusting relationships that support growth, development, and learning.	Model changing a diaper and feeding a young infant with an emphasis on talking and engaging with the child. Afterward discuss what you did and why. Point out how the child responded to your interactions. Then observe the teacher doing these routines and ask him or her to do a self-critique.
Babies cry frequently and for long periods of time; teachers say, "They're just spoiled."	Teachers may only know one or two ways to soothe a crying baby. If these approaches do not work, they give up, sometimes blaming the baby. Perhaps they follow a strict schedule and think it is not time for the baby to sleep or be fed. It is possible they think that crying infants are spoiled and need to learn how to wait patiently.	Suggest that teachers ask families to share the strategies they use at home to calm their babies. Teachers can also observe the techniques their colleagues use to help crying babies feel better. Visit the classroom frequently to make sure babies' needs are met promptly and consistently. Explain that babies can't be spoiled, repeating this message as often as needed.
Mobile infants climb on the shelves to look out the window.	There are lots of fascinating things outside that the infants want to see. The shelves sit in front of the window and thus, invite children to climb.	Help teachers find another place for the shelves. Provide a carpeted platform or a sturdy stepstool big enough for two so children can have a safe perch from which to observe the outside world.

Warning sign	Why this might be happening	How educators can address the problem
Mobile infants cry from frustration when they can't express themselves.	Mobile infants may know exactly what they want, but they don't have the language or social skills needed to make verbal requests. Teachers may not have understood the children's nonverbal gestures.	Help teachers practice observing and responding to mobile infants' cues. A co-observation could be effective. For example, if a child looks toward something, the child is probably asking for help getting the item. The simple raised-arms gesture is another way this age group seeks attention. "Please pick me up." Teachers can gently remind children who are starting to talk to use their words—at a beginning level—to express their desires.
Families spend little time at the program during drop-off and pickup times.	Teachers may be unfriendly to families or may focus on what children did "wrong" during the day. Families may feel unwelcome and unappreciated.	Observe drop-off and pickup times to see how teachers and families exchange information about a child's day. Note what teachers say to families and how they respond. Share your observations with teachers and jointly plan ways to establish meaningful partnerships with families for the benefit of children and adults.
Teachers isolate mobile infants who pull hair or bite other children.	The children might be curious about a classmate's hair or exploring the use of fine-motor muscles. At this age, children might bite because they explore everything with their mouths. Many teachers—and adults in general—are particularly horrified by these behaviors.	Help teachers understand that in most cases, mobile infants are not trying to hurt each other. Lead teachers in practicing appropriate responses to the child who accidentally hurts another as well as to the child who got hurt. A baby who pulls hair can learn to gently stroke the hair instead. A child who bites could feel crowded or may need a cold, wet washcloth to bite instead.
Teachers harshly reprimand or even punish infants; they often expect infants to stop behaviors that are typical for their age and stage of development, such as dropping things on the floor or grabbing toys from each other.	Teachers may have unrealistic expectations for infants' behavior and believe infants can use self-control. They may lack an understanding of child development and may not know how to use positive guidance strategies.	Plan to include discussions about child development as part of weekly teachers meetings. Share information in bite-size pieces so it is easier to absorb and apply in practice. Visit classrooms and model positive guidance so teachers can see what to do and how it succeeds as a teaching strategy. Ensure that teachers know it is never okay to reprimand or punish the children in their care.

3 Ensuring the Effectiveness of Toddler Programs

A high-quality program for toddlers provides a balance between a toddler's conflicting needs for security and independence. Teachers respond to toddlers' struggles to become independent by allowing them to make simple choices and to do things for themselves. Teachers offer safety and comfort to children who are distressed and provide support as toddlers attempt new tasks. Children do many of the same things at the program that they do at home with their families, such as looking at books, scribbling on paper, and eating together. And because most toddlers are energy in action, they have ample opportunities to climb, run, crawl, and move around.

You can use the information and guidance in this chapter to oversee the toddler environment, toys, materials, and equipment, program structure, curriculum, supportive interactions, and positive guidance. The exact age range covered by the toddler years varies from program to program and publication to publication due to the different rates of individual children's growth, development, and learning. In this book, we define toddlerhood as being from sixteen to thirty-six months.

This chapter includes the following sections:

☀ Environment, pages 58–64

☀ Toys, Materials, and Equipment, pages 64–72

☀ Program Structure, pages 72–78

☀ Curriculum: Activities and Experiences, pages 78–84

☀ Supportive Interactions, pages 84–89

☀ Positive Guidance, pages 90–95

Environment

The starting point for overseeing and maintaining a high-quality toddler program is having a physical environment that is designed to facilitate growth, development, and learning for this age group. Indeed, the program design is a blueprint for curriculum implementation. It also creates a physical and social atmosphere that reflects your program's philosophy and enables teachers to support individual and group progress.

Foundations Underlying Quality

Before observing the effectiveness of the program environment, you will need to be sure certain baseline standards for quality are being met. These standards include the size of the indoor and outdoor settings, health and safety measures, and how the setting is arranged to support children and teachers.

Program Space

Toddler programs are housed in a wide variety of dedicated or adapted spaces, ranging from classrooms to trailers to church facilities. Standards for indoor space are set by federal (in the case of Early Head Start and military child development), state, local, and tribal licensing authorities and will vary, so you need to check your own licensing agency for governing requirements on square footage. Early Head Start programs, for example, have to comply with applicable state, tribal, or local licensing regulations but must provide a minimum of thirty-five square feet per child, exclusive of space for toileting, storage, and built-in furnishings (Office of Head Start 2017).

Because the amount of space directly correlates with quality, exceeding these requirements can benefit children. *Caring for Our Children*, a compilation of health and safety performance standards issued jointly by the American Academy of Pediatrics, the American Public Health Association, and the National Resource Center for Health and Safety in Child Care and Early Education, notes that "historically, a standard of thirty-five square feet was used. Recommendations from research studies range between forty-two to fifty-four square feet per child. Child behavior tends to be more constructive when sufficient space is organized to promote developmentally appropriate skills. Crowding has been shown to be associated with increased risk of developing upper respiratory infections. Also, having sufficient space will reduce the risk of injury from simultaneous activities" (American Academy of Pediatrics 2011, 203). *Caring for Our Children* recommends a minimum of forty-two square feet per child but suggests that fifty square feet of usable floor space is "preferred" (American Academy of Pediatrics 2011).

The space designated for outdoor play and learning includes soil, sand, grass, hills, and flat, hard surfaces. Toddler outdoor spaces should be adjacent to but separate from infant outdoor play areas. This is because active toddlers, who are always on the move, might accidentally knock down or trip over smaller children.

Federal, state, local, and tribal regulations on appropriate square footage for outdoor environments vary. However, *Caring for Our Children* recommends at least fifty square feet of accessible outdoor play space per toddler up to two years of age and seventy-five square feet of space per toddler ages two and above (American Academy of Pediatrics 2011).

Health and Safety

Before supervisors can effectively monitor how the environment supports children and teachers, the setting must be checked to ensure it is a safe and healthy place for children to play. For toddlers, who seem to be in perpetual motion, this is especially important. Your local, state, or tribal licensing agency issues mandatory health and safety guidelines. Early Head Start and military child development programs have stringent standards for health and safety requirements.

To ensure that your program's environment complies with indoor and outdoor health and safety requirements, we have included a checklist in appendix A. Though not all-inclusive, this checklist reflects Early Head Start and military child development programs. Once you are assured that children are safe and healthy, you can concentrate on how the environment facilitates toddlers' growth and development.

Room / Outdoor Space Arrangement

Best practices in the toddler years include arranging the setting into spaces to accommodate children's routines and learning experiences, keeping in mind their active lifestyle. A well-planned and supportive setting for toddlers includes the following:

* a family greeting space where family members sign in and teachers communicate and exchange information with families about each child's daily routines and activities at home and at the program

* cubbies for storing personal items from home

* a well-stocked diapering area/bathroom with child-size toilets and sinks

* an eating/snacking/cooking area with child-size table and chairs

* space for playing with toys, with child-size table and chairs

* space for doing art, with easels and child-size table and chairs

* construction area, with block props

* space for pretending and dressing up

* space for looking at / listening to books and "writing"

* space for sand and water play, with props and waterproof smocks

* space for dancing to music, climbing, sliding, and doing other gross-motor activities

* places where children can be by themselves and recharge

Outdoor places for toddlers need to be inviting, exciting, and large enough to let them develop the many gross-motor skills they are learning to master—running, leaping, galloping, prancing, and dancing, among others. They also need space to do the following activities:

- push and pull toys, carriages, and wagons

- climb on platforms and low (eighteen inches or less) climbers

- slide

- swing

- walk on a balance beam

- throw, catch, and kick balls

- swing on ropes

- pedal wheeled toys and trikes

- play at sand and water tubs

- look at books and do other quiet activities

- draw or paint

- engage in pretend play

- build with blocks

What the Environment Should Look Like

An appropriate environment for toddlers includes several small, clearly defined interest areas, as described above, where two or three toddlers can engage in activities such as playing with water or sand, fingerpainting, building with large cardboard blocks, or hopping to music like bunnies. Teachers arrange the furniture and equipment so that toddlers have plenty of room to move about and use their large muscles. To ensure smooth, safe operations, the toddler room is set up so that teachers can see what is happening in all parts of the room. Family members should always be welcome in the toddler room, with an area set aside for teacher-family communications. Listed below are examples of what you should see in a center-based program serving toddlers and why these arrangements of the environment are important.

What you should see	Why
A welcoming area for families that offers opportunities for family members to talk with teachers, for teachers to leave information for families about their children and the program, and for both families and teachers to share resources on parenting and other topics.	Families and teachers need to support each other as they respond to toddlers' conflicting needs to be independent and to stay in close touch with familiar people and experiences. Daily interactions help all adults plan an appropriate program that meets individual needs.
Photographs of the children are prominently displayed in their cubbies and throughout the classroom. Photos of the children with their families are posted in the classroom and in "All about Me" books in the library area.	Displaying photographs of children helps them develop a sense of belonging. Family photos enable children, especially those who have trouble separating, to "keep in touch" with their families during the day. Children feel valued and special when they see their family as part of the program.
Materials throughout the program reflect the children's backgrounds. (For example, books, dolls, wooden people props, dress-up clothes, music, food props and real foods served at snack and in cooking activities reflect each child's culture and family structure.)	Children feel a sense of inclusion and trust when they see themselves and their culture reflected in program materials. Children who feel valued for who they are become eager to learn.
Flooring textures, tape, and furniture, such as child-size room dividers, are used to designate interest areas in the room.	Dividing the space into interest areas helps children identify where they can play with toys, build with blocks, paint a picture, or try on a firefighter's outfit. When all related materials and props are housed together, toddlers can make independent choices. Interest areas are places where toddlers can safely explore and experiment at will.
Messy activities like cooking, art, and sand/water play take place on washable flooring, while blocks, dramatic play, music, and literacy take place on carpeted floors.	Children need to be free to create with abandon. Having washable flooring allows them to be creatively messy during art, cooking, and sand and water play. Carpeting in areas that are not likely to be messy zones allows toddlers to be comfortable sitting on the floor for block play and cozy while lying down to look at a book.
Low, open shelving stocked with toys/materials and containers labeled with pictures and words in English and the home languages spoken by children. Duplicates of the children's favorite playthings are placed near each other on the shelves.	Toddlers are trying hard to be independent and to feel competent. Low, open shelving with labels with both pictures and words allow children to select and return toys without asking for assistance. Having duplicates of toys avoids squabbles, since most toddlers are not yet developmentally capable of sharing.

What you should see	Why
Personal areas such as cubbies and "be by myself" spaces (for example, lofts or large cardboard boxes lined with blankets and pillows) that are visible to teachers.	Some children find the noise and activity level in the toddler room overwhelming. Personal spaces allow children to be alone or observe the action from afar while recouping their energy and managing their emotions. Private spaces also let children know that their privacy is respected. Teachers, of course, need to see all children at all times to provide proper supervision.
An easily sanitized diapering area that is regularly stocked with supplies and has a foot-operated trash can lined with a plastic bag and sturdy steps so older toddlers can climb up to the table on their own.	Many toddlers are still in diapers. A well-planned diapering area where teachers have what they need at hand allows them to interact with and build reciprocal relationships with children during diapering. Toddlers can also participate in the diapering process by climbing up on the table and washing their hands themselves.
Child-size toilets and sinks located in a bathroom adjacent to the classroom or one in a nearby hallway that children use with adult supervision.	Some toddlers from about the age of two are toilet trained or in the process of becoming toilet trained. Children can use a bathroom somewhat independently and learn important self-help skills such as washing their hands. When the bathroom is in the hall, children likewise use it independently but with adult supervision.
Large, open spaces containing ramps, steps, and other equipment that encourage physical activity.	Fast-growing toddlers are filled with energy. They need many opportunities to use their gross-motor skills. Because they cannot confine their running, jumping, and climbing to the times they are outdoors, they need indoor space and equipment that facilitate active play.
Indoor spaces large enough for two or three children to play side by side.	Toddlers are social beings and enjoy being close to friends. They may not be developmentally able to play interactively with others, but they enjoy playing alongside other children in parallel play.
The outdoor area has designated active play spaces for individuals or small groups of children (for example, playing on swings, slides, and climbers; throwing balls; using riding toys; doing construction; gardening; observing animals; creating art; and playing with sand and water).	Toddlers have boundless energy. They need large spaces to practice and master use of large muscles. They also need places to explore and experiment with nature through art, sand, water, and gardening activities. This helps them develop cognitive and socio-emotional skills, as well as physical ones.

When the twelve items noted above are in place, the environment is likely to support toddlers' growth, development, and learning. Use the checklist in appendix C to observe how well your program meets these criteria. For items that your program is not yet addressing well, work with teachers to devise and implement an action plan for improvement. As a supervisor, you are responsible for ensuring that all components of the indoor and outdoor environment are optimally serving children and teachers.

When the Environment Needs Further Adjusting

For deeper insight into the effectiveness of the environment, it's important to observe how children use the indoor and outdoor spaces. It's one thing to have an environment that is well-designed and laid out, but unless children are using it as planned, it will not serve the program well. If you spot children engaged in behaviors such as those described below, the environment may be contributing to problems that hamper their progress. Discuss the possible solutions noted in the third column with teachers and help them implement these countermeasures, if appropriate.

Note: Some of the warning signs listed below may be caused by factors other than the environment or by a combination of environmental and other factors. Regular observations will provide information about the cause of the problem.

Warning sign	Why this might be happening	How educators can address the problem
Toddlers break down into tears during the day for no apparent reason.	There are not enough personal spaces for children to "take a break" from the group action.	In corners, a loft, or a nook of the room, teachers can provide pillows and other soft, cozy furnishings for children to be comfortably alone when they need to retreat from the group.
Toddlers climb on tables and other furniture despite teachers' frequent reminders.	There is not enough space or equipment for children to develop their gross-motor skills while indoors.	Brainstorm with teachers about how to encourage gross-motor play in the classroom. Add climbing or sliding equipment, or, if there is not enough space indoors for children to exercise their developing muscles, add another outdoor play period.
Toddlers move and engage in gross-motor activities but are not playing with toys and materials.	In an effort to provide enough space for gross-motor activities, shelving has been pushed against the walls and activity areas are no longer defined.	Work with teachers to rearrange the room to create interest areas where children engage in art, reading, constructing, and sand/water play. Place labeled toys and props on low shelving where children can access them easily.
Toddlers often ask teachers for materials they want to use. (For example, paper to go with crayons or a colander for water play.)	Materials that go with each other, such as paper and crayons, are not grouped together on shelving in the area where they will be used.	Encourage teachers to group materials together that are used together. Place all art materials near a table and chairs. Similarly, group pretend-play props in one place, close to the construction area. This will enable children to find all the materials they need for an activity and use them independently.

Warning sign	Why this might be happening	How educators can address the problem
Toddlers rarely use some of the interest areas that used to be popular.	Toddlers change interests and gain new skills rapidly. What was popular a few weeks ago may no longer be appropriate.	Encourage teachers to observe and listen to children to learn about their current skills and interests. Work with teachers to rotate materials and props and add new ones that are more appropriate for individuals and the group.
Children spend little time looking at books and quickly move on to another activity.	Quiet activities may be located next to noisy ones so the children in the literacy area are distracted by nearby activities.	Review the room arrangement with teachers. Examine how furniture might be rearranged to separate noisy activities like block play from quiet activities like looking at a book.
Mealtime noise levels are too loud for conversation.	Teachers push tables together at mealtimes and have all children eat in a large group instead of at separate small tables. Teachers have inappropriate expectations for toddlers.	Review with teachers effective strategies for family-style dining with toddlers. Encourage teachers to plan for no more than five children at a table with an adult who can lead the children in conversation.
During outdoor play, children fall off of the climbing equipment and often need help getting on the swings.	The program may lack a dedicated outdoor area for this age group. The equipment used by the toddlers is designed for preschoolers and/or school-age children. Using this equipment with younger children is both frustrating and dangerous.	Designate a specific part of the outdoor area for children to do activities that don't involve using equipment designed for older children. Advocate for funding to create a toddler-friendly outdoor play area.

Toys, Materials, and Equipment

The effectiveness of well-designed indoor and outdoor environments is directly dependent on how these areas are stocked with equipment, toys, and materials. High-quality toddler programs contain a rich supply of toys, materials, and equipment appropriate for the ages, stages, abilities, cultures, languages, and other characteristics of the children in the group. They both match and challenge the children's skills and development. Children need to experience success and, at the same time, to be sufficiently challenged to learn new skills and concepts.

Foundations Underlying Quality

Before observing the equipment, toys, and materials in your program's indoor and outdoor environments to ensure their effectiveness, you will need to be sure that certain baseline standards for quality are being met. These concern the developmental appropriateness of your inventory and their adherence to safety.

Selection of Toys, Materials, and Equipment

A high-quality program for toddlers should be stocked with toys, materials, and equipment that support children's growth, development, and learning, including their increasing needs for independence, initiative, and interactions. Therefore, there needs to be a wide range of choices so every child in the group has something interesting to play with.

Because every program, and the children and families served, has unique characteristics, no one master inventory is appropriate for all toddler classrooms. Your choices should reflect the cultures, home languages and families of the children in the group, as well as your budget. In addition, if children in your program have special needs, the inventory needs to be supplemented with toys, materials, and equipment that are adapted so all children can fully participate in the program.

The following lists are in no way exhaustive. Rather, these lists are a starting point for checking that your program has an age-appropriate, individually appropriate, and culturally appropriate inventory for toddlers (Dodge, Rudick, and Berke 2011).

TOYS AND MATERIALS

Homey and natural
- pots and pans
- wooden spoons
- plastic bowls and cups
- blankets
- stuffed animals
- pinecones
- shells
- leaves
- plastic bottles
- cardboard boxes with and without lids

Books / language and literacy
- sturdy books with pages children can turn, illustrations they can point to, and characters (human and animal) they can identify with
- puppets and a stage
- writing tools and papers
- photos of toddlers' families, familiar objects, and animals

Manipulative toys
- busy boxes and surprise boxes
- stacking post and rings
- shape-sorting boxes
- nesting boxes/baskets
- large plastic snap beads
- large wooden beads and laces
- lacing cards
- personal care boards and dolls (with zippers, buttons, and Velcro closures)
- containers in graduated sizes (such as plastic bowls or cups)
- pegboards with large holes and pegs
- giant dominoes
- table and floor puzzles with four to thirty pieces (or more), with and without knobs

Construction

☼ unit blocks

☼ cardboard blocks that look like bricks

☼ hollow blocks

☼ multicolored, rectangular, plastic blocks

☼ foam blocks

☼ Duplos or other interlocking blocks

☼ wooden table blocks

☼ alphabet blocks

☼ wooden and plastic people, animals, and traffic signs

Gross-motor development

☼ large cardboard boxes

☼ tunnels

☼ carpeted climbers

☼ carpeted riser/platforms

☼ push and pull toys

☼ transportation toys

☼ beanbags and baskets

☼ balls

Dancing/marching/music

☼ simple rhythm instruments (drums, xylophones, tambourines, maracas, clackers)

☼ bell bracelets and anklets

☼ push and pull toys that make music

☼ balls with bells inside them

☼ music boxes (to wind up or to pull)

☼ CD player with CDs, MP3 player, tablet, or other form of digital music

☼ scarves for waving while dancing or marching

☼ picture books that feature songs and fingerplays

Art

☼ jumbo paintbrushes

☼ tempera paint

☼ various papers (poster, tissue, crepe, cardboard, butcher)

☼ fingerpaints and paper or shallow trays

☼ sponges and toothbrushes for painting

☼ stamp pad and stamps

☼ playdough and molding tools

☼ collage materials (dried flowers, yarn, ribbons, recycled greeting cards, and wrapping paper)

☼ blunt-nosed scissors (older toddlers)

☼ library paste (older toddlers)

☼ jumbo chalk (white and colored)

☼ smocks

Pretend play

☼ dolls (multiethnic)

☼ doll bottles, blankets, and cradle/crib

☼ child-size home furnishings (refrigerator, stove, sink, and so on)

☼ work-related props (firefighter's hat, construction hat, stethoscope, tool belt, and so on)

☼ dress-up clothes

☼ hats, purses, tote bags, backpacks

☼ unbreakable tea set

☼ real or toy telephone

☼ empty food boxes

☼ child-size pots, pans, plastic dishes, and utensils

☼ child-size broom and mop

☼ prop boxes for older toddlers

Snacks and cooking

☼ real spoons and forks

☼ unbreakable plates and bowls

☼ plastic knives

☼ whisk

☼ scrub brush / vegetable brush

☼ wooden spoons

☼ spatulas

☼ trays

☼ small pitchers

- colander
- ladle
- potato masher
- cookie cutters
- sponges
- child-size mop and broom
- picture books on foods and cooking projects/ recipes for children

Sand and water play
- sterilized play sand
- tubs/bins/trays for sand and water
- plastic/rubber people and animals
- cars, boats, and other transportation vehicles
- sand rakes
- shovels
- plastic buckets
- squeeze bottles
- colander/sieve
- scoops
- straws
- cookie cutters
- water/sand mills
- collectibles like shells and pinecones
- smocks

Outdoor play
- plastic containers, cups, bottles, pitchers, pails, and buckets (for sand or water play)
- streamers
- bug boxes
- push and pull toys
- balls
- large plastic or hollow blocks
- beanbags
- sidewalk chalk
- magnifying glass
- boxes

EQUIPMENT

Indoors
- low tables with child-size chairs
- room dividers / low, open shelving
- area rugs
- cots or sleeping mats
- cubbies / storage units
- storage for adult belongings

Outdoors
- bucket swings
- climber
- playhouse
- tunnels
- sterilized play sand and sandbox / sand tub
- water tubs
- riding toys (that can be pushed with feet)
- small tricycles and helmets
- gardening equipment (trowels, rakes)
- balls and bats (made of plastic or foam)

SAFETY REMINDERS

All the equipment, materials, and toys in your program must meet these safety requirements:

- be free of sharp edges, splinters, lead paint, and other toxins
- pose no potential choking or suffocation hazards
- meet applicable safety guidelines issued by local, state, or tribal licensing agencies, Early Head Start, or military child development programs

Use the safety checklist in appendix A to ensure that the toys, materials, and equipment in your program are safe for toddlers.

What Toys, Materials, and Equipment Should Look Like

In a high-quality toddler program, the toys, materials, and equipment in the indoor and outdoor spaces should be varied, developmentally appropriate, and inviting. In the following examples, you will see what quality measures should be in place when you observe the toys, materials, and equipment in a toddler program and why these measures are important.

What you should see	Why
Toddlers' personal items from home (such as blankets and stuffed animals), homelike items like cushions, a tablecloth, plants, culturally significant props and play materials, and books, print, music, and other items in children's home languages.	Since toddlers feel most secure at home with their families, creating a homelike atmosphere in the classroom fosters a sense of security. Personal items and materials found at home send children a message that this is a place where they can trust that they will be safe. Including home languages supports toddlers' language development and links them to home and family.
Books about families, everyday experiences, animals, and simple concepts like color and shape, numbers, and the alphabet. Books have colorful illustrations and have few words on a page or are wordless. There are books in English and children's home languages.	Reading picture books, in English and home languages, that interest the children stimulates language development and sets the stage for reading. Teachers can read to children daily by themselves, with another child, or in a small group. Toddlers can also look at books by themselves.
Blocks (soft, cardboard, and wooden) and accessories such as wooden animals, people, traffic signs, and vehicles.	Toddlers use blocks to build, sort, pretend, and practice their fine- and gross-motor skills. Props further stimulate imaginative play.
Materials that allow toddlers to pretend and take on roles (for example, dress-up clothes and props, baby dolls with cribs and high chairs, and a prop box for a doctor's office).	Toddlers' imaginative play, alone or with a few other children, is about real experiences they have observed or participated in at home, in their community, or at the program. Their play typically focuses on family life—cooking, cleaning, leaving and returning home, caring for babies or pets, or driving a car. Pretend play helps toddlers understand life, follow rules, and play with others.
Beanbags, small blocks, and pinecones and containers such as baskets, boxes, and pails.	Toddlers are enthralled with filling and dumping activities. Through repeated successes, children learn about space and volume. This activity is also a favorite because it gives children a much-desired sense of control over their environment.
Art materials that allow children to draw, paint (including fingerpainting), mold doughs, print, and make collages.	Toddlers enjoy the process of art—filling paper with paint strokes, poking a hole in playdough, and making bold lines with chalk on a chalkboard. Art materials give children an opportunity to express their feelings and emotions as they learn to control their brushstrokes and scribbles.

What you should see	Why
Rhythm instruments (both purchased and homemade), musical toys and balls, and devices such as CD players, MP3 players, or tablets for listening to and making music.	Toddlers are naturally drawn to music, which lays a foundation for patterning and math. Children love to move to music, play along with their own rhythm instruments, and sing songs.
Materials such as pegboards, puzzles, dominoes, and lacing beads that encourage problem solving and other cognitive skills.	Toddlers develop thinking skills as they manipulate objects and see how they work. When they successfully put together a ten-piece puzzle, they learn about the relationship of parts to the whole, about shape and number, and about perspective. They also refine fine-motor skills, learn patience, and experience pride in their accomplishments.
Wheeled toys (such as wagons and trucks) that toddlers can ride, push, and pull, and equipment (for example, climbers, a rocking boat, or slide) for use in gross-motor activities.	Most toddlers are constantly on the move, using their whole bodies to learn. Participating in physical activities allows toddlers to develop new motor skills and to refine old ones. Large-muscle activities like climbing, sliding, jumping, or rocking give children a chance to feel control over their environment.
Natural materials that children can explore and manipulate, such as sand and water, leaves, shells, and plants.	Sensory experiences with natural items are soothing to young children. They also promote cognitive development as children observe what happens after they splash water or uncover a toy dinosaur buried in the sand.
Unbreakable dishes, flatware, utensils, bowls, and kitchen gadgets are accessible to children.	Toddlers enjoy feeding themselves as they sit at a child-size table with others. Toddlers can also take an active role in preparing foods as they whisk eggs, slice a banana, and snap the ends off green beans. These activities help children learn about nutrition, develop fine-motor skills, and teach concepts such as cause and effect, number, color, and shape.
Equipment and materials that promote gross-motor activity and interaction with nature (for example, swings, slides, climbers, sand and water tubs/boxes, a playhouse, a tire, tunnels, and a garden).	Toddlers need to be outdoors every day to experience sensory and physical development. Slides, climbers, and tunnels enable children to refine their large-muscle skills that are developing at a quick pace. All toddlers benefit from being in the wind and sun and observing plants, flowers, trees, bugs, birds, and worms.

When you observe the twelve items noted above in place, it is likely that the equipment, toys, and materials in your program support toddlers' learning. Use the checklist in appendix C to observe how well your program meets these criteria. For items that your program is not yet addressing well, work with teachers to devise and implement an action plan for improvement. As a supervisor, you are responsible for ensuring that program materials and equipment optimally support children's growth, development, and learning.

When the Toys, Materials, and Equipment Need Further Adjusting

For deeper insight into the effectiveness of your program's equipment and materials, it's important to observe children using the materials. It's one thing to have a well-thought-out inventory of safe and developmentally appropriate toys, materials, and equipment, but unless children are using these items in ways that facilitate growth, development, and learning, they are of little use. If you spot children engaged in behaviors such as those described below, the equipment, toys, and materials may be contributing to problems that hamper learning. Discuss with teachers the warning sign, reasons why the behavior might be happening, and the possible solutions noted in the third column. Help them implement these countermeasures or others they develop to make your program's toys, materials, and equipment more effective.

Note: Some of the warning signs listed below may be caused by factors other than the program's equipment, toys, and materials or by a combination of the program's equipment, toys, and materials and other factors. Regular observations will provide information about the precise cause of the problem.

Warning sign	Why this might be happening	How educators can address the problem
Toddlers run around in circles during outdoor playtime while teachers encourage them to let off steam.	Most toddlers are whirlwinds of energy, and outdoor time does provide opportunities to expend this energy. However, being outside offers other important learning opportunities that teachers need to take advantage of.	Meet with teachers to review the goals for outdoor play. Suggest props to bring outdoors for pretend play or sand and water play. Discuss activities such as helping children search for ladybugs and other insects, planting and tending a garden, and taking nature walks with toddlers.
Children at play in the home area walk across the classroom to get needed props, such as magazines or cooking utensils, frequently grabbing those items from other children who are using them.	The props for pretend play are not located near each other. Teachers may believe that all books and magazines should be in one place and all cooking utensils should be stored where children have snacks and tasting experiences.	Explain to teachers that it is fine to display books and magazines in the reading area and utensils in the snacking area. However, ask them to add a few books, magazines, and cooking utensils to the home area to enhance toddlers' play. Because toddlers are easily frustrated, it's best to have everything they need for an activity at hand. This proactive approach prevents behavior problems, such as a child grabbing an item from a classmate.

Warning sign	Why this might be happening	How educators can address the problem
Children fidget after just a few minutes of group time and run throughout the classroom.	Children haven't had enough opportunities to use the gross-motor equipment and materials either indoors or outdoors.	Toddlers have an innate need to move. Go over daily plans with the teachers and ensure the schedule offers enough time for morning and afternoon gross-motor activities.
Children play near each other on the floor and fight over who gets the fire truck and other toys.	Teachers think that it is important for toddlers to learn how to share. They may not know that toddlers have not yet developed the skills that will one day allow them to share without concern.	Emphasize to teachers that toddlers are not developmentally capable of sharing. Have them keep track of which items are used most often so they can offer duplicates (or triplicates) of popular items—such as fire trucks. This will avoid many disagreements among toddlers.
Children look for teachers to hand them the toys they want to play with.	Materials are not accessible to children. Or teachers want to control what materials the toddlers use.	Discuss with teachers the importance of encouraging toddlers' independence by letting them get out materials on their own. Also underscore that children are more likely to be engaged when they—not someone else—select play materials. Ask teachers to make sure toys and materials are appropriately displayed on low shelving with labels.
Toddlers wait for teachers to help them use toys, materials, or equipment; they express their frustration by being cranky or crying.	The classroom does not have enough items that children can use independently. Or teachers will not let children use items on their own because they are afraid they will get broken.	Work with teachers to sort toys, materials, and equipment into two categories: items children can use without adult assistance and items children need adult assistance to use. If most of the items fall into the second category, help teachers select and display new playthings that children can use independently.
Children throw toys and materials on the floor and leave the interest area seeking something else to do.	Children are bored, having lost interest in playing with a specific toy or material over and over. Perhaps there are not enough props to make the activity continually interesting. Additionally, children don't know the cleanup rules or don't know how to clean up after playing.	Help teachers to create a system for regularly rotating toys and materials in response to children's changing interests and abilities. Ask them to review the inventory to make sure the available props enrich and extend children's play. Also, brainstorm with teachers ways to help children learn how and where to return items they are no longer using. Make sure there is adequate, well-labeled space on shelves for housing toys and materials.

Warning sign	Why this might be happening	How educators can address the problem
Children get upset when invited to join others who are fingerpainting at the art table.	A number of children—especially those on the autism spectrum—have what is known as sensory defensiveness and don't like the feel or touch of certain art materials, especially paints.	Invite a special educator to meet with teachers and discuss the issue. The most important thing is that teachers be respectful of the children's sensitivity and not force them to participate. As an alternative to fingerpainting, teachers could place some paint in a sealable plastic bag and have the child etch designs with a finger on top of the bag. Alternatively, many children with sensitivity issues are fine using markers as a painting substitute.

Program Structure

The program structure provides the framework for the day's events. When followed consistently, this structure gives children a sense of security and a feeling of control as they master the order in which events take place. A toddler might think, "We just had lunch, so now we will wash our hands and brush our teeth. Then we will have naps." The time allocated for each segment of the schedule should reflect a recognition of toddlers' individual needs, interests, and abilities. Above all, the schedule for a toddler room needs to be flexible.

Foundations Underlying Quality

Before observing your program's structure to ensure its effectiveness, you will need to be sure your program's schedule is appropriate for toddlers and has an effective approach to carrying out transitions.

Sample Schedule for a Toddler Program

A schedule for toddlers needs to recognize that children sometimes have conflicting desires to be secure with a trusted teacher, assert their independence, do things for themselves, and socially eat and interact with their peers. In addition, quiet times should alternate with active ones, outdoor play should occur every day, and full group times should be brief. Other than these few commonalities, toddler schedules tend to vary to meet the developmental need of each child, which can differ greatly at this age.

Because of this variability, several activities are usually taking place at the same time. The schedule that follows, which is designed for a full-day program, is offered as a sample (Dodge, Rudick, and Berke 2011). It should be adjusted to accommodate the needs of the toddlers your program serves.

Scheduled activity	Approximate length of time	What teachers do
Teacher planning time	30 minutes prior to opening	Review the day's plans, conduct health and safety checks, make sure all needed materials are out and available to children. Wash hands.
Arrival and settling in	45 minutes	Greet individual children and family members. Exchange information with family members. Help children take off and store jackets. Check diapers of children who are not toilet trained, and have toilet-trained children use the bathroom. Help children wash hands upon arrival and before eating breakfast (if applicable).
Indoor playtime	60 minutes	Encourage children to select playthings and assist as needed. Support children's play and ask questions to extend learning. Change diapers as needed; accompany children to toilet. Help children wash hands and eat morning snack either individually or with others. Help children put on outerwear, depending on the temperature, before going outside.
Outdoor playtime	60 minutes	Supervise and interact with children as they explore, use slides and swings, and engage with other play materials and equipment.
Lunchtime	45 minutes	Help children take off and store outerwear. Check diapers and accompany children to toilets. Help everyone wash hands. Sit with children in small groups as they eat lunch. Help children with hand washing and toothbrushing after eating.
Naptime	90–120 minutes, depending on length of program day and individual needs	Set up mats/cots and help children prepare for sleep. Allow children to sleep until they individually wake up. Check diapers and take children to toilet upon awakening. Help children brush hair and wash hands.
Indoor or outdoor play	45 minutes	As children wake up, offer a snack. Read and sing to children. Help children choose activities and interact with them.
Departure	15 minutes	Check diapers and take children to toilet as needed. Wash hands. Greet children's families individually and help them reconnect with their children. Assist families with taking home child's work and soiled items. Exchange information about the child's day. Make sure to say something special about each child.
Debriefing	30 minutes or as time allows	Review the day, work on children's portfolios, and plan for the next day.

Transitions

Transitions are the in-between times when children move from one activity to the next—from indoor to outdoor activities, from outdoor play to lunch preparation and lunchtime, from lunchtime to rest time, and the like. With toddlers, the day is heavy with transitions. Transitions can become problem periods if children don't know what is expected. Waiting is difficult for young children, and unless they are engaged in something interesting, they might find something to do that does not fit in with the teachers' plans.

To make transitions easier, teachers can plan for them. Here are some ideas on how to do this:

- **Be organized.** If you are going to change diapers or take children to the bathroom, make sure everything you need is at hand.

- **Avoid having children wait around.** For example, one teacher can interact with toddlers playing while another teacher takes a small group to put on their jackets to go outside.

- **Give clear, age-appropriate directions.** "Take a paper towel to wipe your hands, please."

- **Point out what comes next** in the day by pointing to a picture schedule illustrated with photos of the children engaged in each activity.

- **Give children a warning** that a transition is about to take place: "It's almost time to go outside. Please finish up playing with your toys now."

- **Use visual cues.** Hold up a backpack to alert children that it's time to go home.

- **Be flexible.** If children are happily engaged in painting the side of the building with water, give them time to finish up before going back indoors.

What Program Structure Should Look Like

In a high-quality program, the program structure supports and enhances children's growth, development, and learning. The daily schedule allows children to become deeply involved in activities and to transition from quiet to active play. Routines and transitions are integrated into learning activities. Everything that happens during the day supports children's growth, development, and learning.

In the chart below, you will find examples of an appropriate program structure and how it supports toddlers' progress.

What you should see	Why
Teachers and children refer to a picture/ photograph schedule illustrating the sequence of the day's activities. The schedule is at toddlers' eye level.	Toddlers develop a sense of trust and feelings of security when they can predict what comes next during the day. Having a picture schedule they can point to provides them with a concrete tool for following the daily events.
Time slots for daily activities match children's developmental capabilities.	Ensuring scheduled time slots match children's developmental abilities reduces the likelihood of behavior problems. For example, most toddlers cannot sit with a group to hear a book or sing a song for longer than five to ten minutes. A longer time slot would likely lead to children being bored, losing focus, or fidgeting.
Active and quiet times are alternated throughout the day. For example, indoor child choice time is followed by physically active time outdoors.	Young children learn through both quiet and physically active play. An appropriate schedule alternates these times so children can recoup the energy expended during gross-motor play by doing quiet activities. Once refreshed, children feel renewed and are eager to engage in active play again.
Children play outdoors at least once a day for at least an hour.	For toddlers whose physical development is virtually exploding, being outdoors every day is crucial to children's health and learning. An hour-long outdoor time allows children to become fully engaged in activities.
Children spend at least an hour engaged in activities of their own choosing and interacting with teachers.	Children learn best when they can select activities that are of interest to them and when they have time to investigate, explore, and experiment. Children can develop increasingly complex thinking skills when they have time to fully interact with materials and people.
Teachers wait patiently as toddlers put on and fasten their own coats, put on their own mittens, get blankets from their cubbies, wipe the table after lunch, and so on.	Participating in routines and transitions is an important part of a toddler's day. Children this age have a great need to do things for themselves and become independent. When teachers build time into the schedule for children to learn and practice self-help skills, they show respect for children's growth, development, and learning.
Teachers lead small-group activities, such as reading a book aloud, marching in a band, or making handprints with paint on poster board.	Toddlers enjoy being with others but cannot manage being with a full group for very long. Keeping the groups small, with two to three children, allows teachers to meet developmental needs while providing individual attention and interaction.
Toddlers regularly nap after lunch and get out their own blankets and lovies from home.	Following a predictable routine at naptime helps toddlers settle down and get needed rest. Having special items from home provides extra security.

What you should see	Why
Children sleep for as long as they need at naptime.	Toddlers have varying needs for sleep. Some will just rest, while others may snooze for a couple of hours. Rather than arouse all children when most have awoken, it's important to let the children get the sleep they need.
Teachers announce to children when a transition is about to take place. For example, "It's almost time to come in for lunch. Let's start putting away our playthings now."	Toddlers can become very involved in activities and find it difficult to stop and change directions. Transitions are smoother and children are more likely to cooperate when they are given a warning and have time to complete what they have started.
Teachers are flexible about the schedule. For example, one might wait to go outside until a crying child is calmed down and ready to put on his jacket. Or the group stays outdoors an extra ten minutes because the children are excitedly blowing and chasing bubbles.	Toddler behavior can be unpredictable. A flexible schedule allows teachers to meet individual and group needs.
Teachers take a small group of toddlers for an impromptu walk around the program—indoors or outdoors.	While predictability is important, sometimes an unplanned activity or a change of scenery is just what's needed to experience new opportunities to learn about the world.

When you observe the twelve items noted above in place, it is likely that your program's schedule is serving toddlers well. Use the checklist in appendix C to observe how well your program meets these criteria. For items that your program is not yet addressing well, work with teachers to devise and implement an action plan for improvement. As a supervisor, you are responsible for ensuring that the program structure optimally supports children's growth, development, and learning.

When the Program Structure Needs Further Adjusting

For deeper insight into the effectiveness of your program's structure, it's important to observe children and teachers throughout the entire day. It's one thing to have a well-thought-out schedule on paper, but unless the schedule allows children the time they need to be involved in activities and to transition smoothly from one activity to the next, it is of little use. If you spot children and teachers engaged in behaviors such as those described below, the program structure may need adjusting. Discuss with teachers the warning sign, reasons why the behavior might be happening, and the possible solutions noted in the third column. Help them implement these countermeasures or others they develop to make your program's structure more effective.

Note: Some of the warning signs listed below may be caused by factors other than the program's structure or by a combination of program structure problems and other factors. Regular observations will provide information about the precise cause of the problem.

Warning sign	Why this might be happening	How educators can address the problem
Children seem confused about what comes next during the day and resist transitioning to the next activity.	There is only a written schedule posted that children cannot read. Or teachers do not prepare children for an upcoming change of activity.	Encourage teachers to take photos of the children during daily routines and activities and use them to make picture schedules to hang at the children's eye level. Work with the teachers to plan how to introduce and refer to the schedule to show children what comes next each day. They can use the photo schedule to help children develop a sense of time and sequencing. In addition, help teachers plan special songs or transition activities. They can use the picture schedule as an aid.
Teachers repeatedly remind children to pay attention at group time. The children wiggle and look around instead of participating, and many leave in search of other activities.	Teachers believe the best way to introduce a new song, concept, or activity is with the full group so that everyone gets the same message. Teachers do not realize this does not work with toddlers who cannot physically be still and concentrate for more than five to ten minutes.	Hold a workshop on effective group times for toddlers. Invite teachers to share ideas for teaching toddlers new songs, concepts, or activities in small groups of two to four children. Later observe teachers at indoor and outdoor playtimes to note how they use small groups. Offer additional support as needed.
Teachers diaper toddlers on demand but have children who are toilet trained use the bathroom only at designated group times.	Teachers may believe that in order to keep to the schedule, children need to use the bathroom en masse. In cases where the children's bathroom is located out of the classroom, teachers may believe that going as a group is safest for the children and minimizes disruption.	Discuss with teachers that while it is appropriate to encourage toilet-trained toddlers to use the bathroom as a group at set times during the day (such as before and after going outdoors, and before and after naps), toddlers—like all of us—need to use the toilet on demand. When the bathroom is out of the classroom, help teachers establish a system for covering for each other when a child needs to be escorted to the bathroom.
Teachers cancel outdoor time on cold days or on hot days. By the end of the morning, children run around the room and get in each other's way.	Children have pent-up energy from being indoors all morning. Teachers do not recognize the importance of going outdoors every day, regardless of the temperature (unless the weather poses a health danger). Perhaps children did not bring clothing that is appropriate for the weather.	Stress the importance of having outdoor time daily. In winter make sure there are plenty of extra mittens, hats, and scarves. If the weather truly becomes too cold or hot to go outdoors, seek out indoor alternatives for gross-motor activity, such as a gym or activity room if there is not a designated gross-motor area in the classroom.

Warning sign	Why this might be happening	How educators can address the problem
Teachers scold children for getting out of line while waiting for their peers to get on their jackets to go outdoors.	Teachers do not handle transitions well. They try to maintain order by having the whole group get ready to go outside at the same time.	Offer print and digital resources with ideas for ensuring smooth transitions for toddlers. Ask teachers to try and report back on effective strategies, such as having only a few children put on their coats at a time. Congratulate teachers when they make transitions fun and successful opportunities to learn.
Teachers perform housekeeping tasks like setting up for lunch, clearing dirty dishes, and setting out and putting away cots, while children restlessly wait for them to finish.	Teachers think this is part of their job and don't believe that toddlers are capable of helping. They might believe, "If I do it myself, it will be faster and more efficient. I won't have to redo what the children do wrong."	Review what toddlers learn and what self-help skills they gain from helping to perform classroom and personal tasks. Ask teachers to review their schedules to make sure they have included time for children to participate in these activities.
Teachers put food on children's plates at mealtime and snacktime and stand over children to make sure they don't make a mess when feeding themselves.	Teachers and/or families may come from a culture in which the norm is to do things for toddlers instead of encouraging them to be independent. They feel that their caregiving is a way of showing love. Teachers may not realize that making a mess is part of children's learning process.	Discuss cultural preferences for when it is and is not appropriate to encourage toddler independence. Review the program's philosophy and approach and agree on goals and expectations. Share resources on how children learn to feed themselves and how children learn independence and personal responsibility when they accomplish this task and others.
Toddlers are unsettled at departure time and search for their belongings to take home.	Teachers don't regard departure time as a distinct part of the schedule. In addition, children are not involved in storing and retrieving their belongings.	After observing the departure time over several days, meet with teachers to discuss the process. As needed, reorganize and label cubbies and storage spaces so that children know where and how to stow their belongings. Suggest establishing some end-of-the-day rituals to help children transition from the program to home.

Curriculum: Activities and Experiences

An early childhood curriculum is a written framework that guides teaching and learning. Like the title of this book, it provides the what, why, and how of implementing a high-quality learning program for young children. Toddler curricula are relationship-based and reflect early learning standards for this age group. They also focus on toddlers' conflicting needs for independence and security.

Foundations Underlying Quality

Before observing teachers implementing the curriculum with toddlers, you will need to be sure your program has a high-quality curriculum in place. Because toddler programs have differing goals and missions, there is no one curriculum that every toddler program should use. Some programs design their own curriculum to meet specific needs and circumstances. Others select and purchase a curriculum such as Teaching Strategies' *The Creative Curriculum for Infants, Toddlers & Twos* or *The HighScope Infant-Toddler Curriculum,* both of which are research-based and validated.

A high-quality toddler curriculum guides teachers, administrators, and families as they work together to support and maximize children's development and learning. Whether program-designed or a standardized commercial one, your curriculum should meet these criteria:

* It is consistent with your program's goals and objectives.

* It is aligned with mandated standards, be they federal (in the case of Early Head Start and military child development programs), state, local, or tribal agency.

* It supports all areas of children's development: emotional, social, physical, language, and cognitive.

* There is documented evidence of the curriculum's success in fostering children's development.

* It is relationship-based; it emphasizes the importance of building relationships among children, teachers, and families.

* It emphasizes using both routines and activities as opportunities to teach and learn.

* It describes how to set up the environment to ensure health, safety, and movement, and it allows for choice.

* The roles and expectations for teachers are described in depth.

* Children have many opportunities to explore the world and experiment through play.

* Learning activities and experiences allow children to play alone, near others, and with others.

* Teaching strategies are differentiated, based on individual skills, abilities, temperaments, interests, learning preferences, home languages, family structures, and cultures.

* It can be tailored to support children with specific disabilities.

* Teachers and families are considered partners in their children's learning at the program and at home.

* Observationally based assessment is used to document children's developmental progress.

What the Curriculum Should Look Like

In a high-quality program, the curriculum is implemented as it was designed to be used. Teachers may make adaptations to fit the makeup of their program, but they adhere to the curriculum's stated goals, objectives, and mission. In the chart below, you will find examples of what the routines and activities in a high-quality toddler curriculum would look like and why.

What you should see	Why
Teachers introduce and reinforce skills based on what they observe children doing and learning. For example, if a teacher observes a child having difficulty placing one block atop another, she looks for other activities that will give the child opportunities to strengthen her fine-motor skills, such as molding with playdough, helping to stir batter in a muffin-making activity, or working on a puzzle.	The teacher's role is to observe toddlers, reflect on what the children are experiencing, and then to provide support and materials that will expand learning. Teachers provide activities and experiences that build on each child's current stage of development, rather than expecting all children to learn the same things at the same time.
Teachers use routines and transitions as opportunities to facilitate learning.	Much of a toddler's day is devoted to routines like eating, dressing, napping, diapering/toileting, and transitioning from one experience to another. Because toddlers are learning from every experience, teachers can capitalize on these experiences as opportunities to sing, talk, get to know children, discuss healthy foods, and play games.
Children work independently on tasks or activities they have selected for themselves. Toddlers might be climbing the steps to the slide, lining up blocks, looking at a book, or filling and dumping things from a container.	When children select an activity of their choice, they are naturally motivated to learn. After observing children's actions, teachers can extend learning by narrating the toddler's actions, asking questions, and offering suggestions; for example, "I see that you've put two of the puzzle pieces in the frame. How will you decide where the other pieces go?"
Children play alongside others. For example, two children may paint at a two-sided easel or wave scarves to music.	Toddlers enjoy the company of their peers but don't yet know how to play cooperatively. Teachers can facilitate the process by encouraging children to play near one another and introducing new social skills.
Teachers regularly observe children's interactions and activities, document what they see and hear, and maintain individual portfolios. Teachers steer children to activities that are a good fit for their observed development and interests.	Observation is a key way to collect the information needed to plan an individualized toddler curriculum that offers opportunities to practice skills a child has mastered and gain new skills. Observations also are used for accountability purposes, to demonstrate success in addressing early learning standards, and to exchange information with families.

What you should see	Why
Children use their large muscles in various activities throughout the day, such as riding scooters outdoors, marching with musical instruments, or stretching to music.	Gross-motor development is a major focus of learning for toddlers. Teachers should engage toddlers in activities both indoors and outdoors that will help them master and develop new movement skills like running, climbing, and throwing.
Children use the small muscles in their hands in various activities throughout the day, such as turning the pages of a book, holding and scribbling with a jumbo crayon, or tearing tissue paper to make a collage.	Fine-motor development is another major focus for toddlers. Teachers should provide materials, experiences, and encouragement to use and develop small muscles.
Children engage in conversations, use language, and see print in English and their home language throughout the day. For example, a toddler might answer a teacher's questions and point to illustrations in a book, show a visitor her name on her cubby, or chime in with a predictable rhyme when singing a song.	Language and early literacy skills develop rapidly during the toddler years. Talking, singing, and observing print and how it is used provide a foundation for later reading and writing. Having print in both English and the children's home languages enables children to retain and gain skills in both languages.
Children solve problems (turn puzzle pieces around to make them fit), explore cause and effect (roll a ball down a ramp), and apply old knowledge to new situations (predict what will happen next when they see the sky turn dark) throughout the day.	Toddlers can build their thinking skills during routines, transitions, and activities. Teachers facilitate cognitive development by providing open-ended materials and interacting with children by narrating the child's actions and results, asking questions, and making suggestions.
Children express their ideas and feelings through the creative arts. For example, toddlers energetically sing a song the teacher has taught them, rock a baby doll to sleep, or make squiggles with washable fingerpaints on a cafeteria tray.	As the Reggio Emilia–based programs have so well demonstrated, the arts provide a springboard for learning. Shaking maracas to the beat of a song, for example, facilitates children's understanding of mathematical patterns. Toddlers can learn other concepts through music, the visual arts, and drama—pretending and using puppets to tell a story.
Teachers ensure that the curriculum is accessible to all children, including those with special needs. For example, teachers check out a book from the library on moving to a new home and read it with a child who is about to move away, allow a child who is sad to sit near them while reading a book to the group, and place raised sandpaper templates on shelving to help a child with visual impairments identify where materials are stored.	Every child has unique strengths and challenges. A high-quality curriculum encourages teachers to modify activities, interactions, and materials as needed to allow all children to fully participate and benefit from the program. This does not mean that each child needs his own curriculum. Rather, it means that the same curriculum needs to be made accessible for each child.

What you should see	Why
Family members share their skills and interests and play with, read to, and otherwise engage the children. For example, a parent reads a book to several children, a grandmother joins her grandson's lunch group, or a parent accompanies the class on a field trip to the zoo.	Research shows that when families partner with early childhood programs, children learn more and feel more competent and confident. It is important that family members feel welcomed by the program and are encouraged to volunteer during the day when children can see them and their teachers working together.

When you observe the twelve items noted above in place, it is likely that your program's curriculum is serving toddlers well. Use the checklist in appendix C to observe how well your program meets these criteria. For items that your program is not yet addressing well, work with teachers to devise and implement an action plan for improvement. As a supervisor, you are responsible for ensuring that the curriculum optimally supports children's growth, development, and learning.

When the Curriculum Needs Further Adjusting

For deeper insight into the effectiveness of your program's curriculum, it's important to observe children and teachers at various times throughout the day. To be fully effective, a high-quality toddler curriculum should be implemented as it was designed to be used, with fidelity. If, for example, your program believes that teachers should speak only English to children whose home language is not English, this would be a misinterpretation of the curriculum's goals and objectives.

Should you spot children and teachers engaged in behaviors such as those described below, the curriculum's implementation may need adjusting. Discuss with teachers the warning sign, reasons why the behavior might be happening, and the possible solutions noted in the third column. Help them implement these countermeasures or others they develop to increase the effectiveness of curriculum implementation.

Note: Some of the warning signs listed below may be caused by factors other than curriculum implementation problems or by a combination of curriculum implementation problems and other factors. Regular observations will provide information about the precise cause of the problem.

Warning sign	Why this might be happening	How educators can address the problem
Toddlers all do the same activity at the same time, such as coloring at tables.	Teachers believe the easiest and most effective approach to teaching is to interest all of the toddlers in the same activity.	With the teachers' permission, video record an activity where everyone is doing the same thing. As a group, critique what is going on. Point out how in actuality this approach is not easy for teachers, as toddlers have a difficult time being in a group—especially when the activity is of no interest to them. Then review with teachers the philosophy behind a toddler curriculum—that teachers need to take their cues from individual children. Discuss how this approach better matches a toddler's skills and development.
The exact same activities take place daily.	Teachers believe that doing the same things every day gives children a sense of order and security.	Provide teachers with print and digital resources on child development and how children learn. At a staff meeting, discuss ways to provide experiences in art, literacy, dramatic play, block building, and so on. Ask teachers to try using a child development-based model in which children rather than teachers make learning choices. Then compare the old and new approaches. Which model do they think leads to more learning?
Teachers direct and lead all of the toddlers' activities.	Teachers think that children learn best when they impart knowledge and show children what to do.	Review with teachers that for toddlers, it is most effective to facilitate learning by allowing children to choose what they want to explore and how they want to approach it. With the teachers' permission, video record them facilitating an activity. Review the footage together with individual teachers so they can see the results of letting children take the lead.
Teachers leave children to play with toys while they sit at a table and plan.	Teachers think that once children are occupied and busy, they can use that time to carry out other responsibilities. Perhaps teachers do not have a dedicated time for planning.	Visit the classroom to model how to interact with children who are playing with toys. Later discuss all the learning opportunities that would have been missed had there been no adult there to interact with the children and guide their focus. Review the work schedule to make sure teachers have sufficient planning time.
Teachers rush through routines, such as putting on / taking off coats, eating meals, and diapering/ toileting.	Teachers believe that all learning occurs during activities and that routines are "downtime."	With the teachers' permission, video record teachers during routines. Then watch the videos individually with each teacher and discuss how she or he might have taken better advantage of these times to support learning. Later make follow-up videos to highlight teachers successfully using routines as opportunities to teach and learn.

Warning sign	Why this might be happening	How educators can address the problem
Children play within stereotypical gender roles—boys play with trucks and trains and girls play with dolls.	Teachers may believe that boys and girls prefer different toys and perhaps subconsciously have steered children to play with toys that they feel are gender appropriate. Teachers and families may come from cultures in which children of all ages are expected to stay within accepted gender roles.	Invite teachers to share their thoughts about gender roles and toys and what they think families believe about this issue. Discuss what messages children learn by trying out different roles, both through toys and in dramatic play. Ask them to reflect on how they might inadvertently send messages about appropriate gender-related behaviors. If it is culturally appropriate, challenge teachers to consciously promote use of all toys and roles by both boys and girls.
Teachers speak only English to children.	Teachers believe that this is the best way for children to learn to speak English. Or teachers are fluent only in English and don't feel competent speaking other languages.	Explain why toddlers who are just learning to speak need to hear the important people in their lives speaking both English and their home language. Encourage teachers to learn a few key words in all of the children's home languages. If teachers have trouble with the pronunciation, try writing typical questions or comments in the children's home languages on sentence strips with a phonetic version underneath. Visitors to the program will find these helpful too.
Children refuse to stay in the group at circle time, even for five to ten minutes.	Teachers expect all toddlers to stay with the group, regardless of individual needs and abilities. Perhaps the group activity is not of interest to some children.	Remind teachers that most toddlers can attend for only five to ten minutes at most. Children who do not feel like participating shouldn't be forced to. Brainstorm appropriate activities that will make group times appealing to the children. Also consider dividing the class in half and holding two circle times, each led by one of the teachers.

Supportive Interactions

In a high-quality toddler program, the teachers demonstrate that they appreciate the special characteristics of toddlers, convey warmth and respect to the children in their care, and support their learning. Interactions are individualized, as when a teacher and toddler wash their hands together and talk about the soap suds. Teachers also interact with small groups, providing directions and useful information to help toddlers stay safe and get involved in the daily program. A teacher might say, "Good morning, Caterpillars. Today we are going to eat lunch outdoors." This simple statement alerts toddlers who need time to adjust to a change in the schedule and gives them a chance to ask questions about the upcoming event.

Foundations Underlying Quality

What kinds of supportive interactions might a visitor to a toddler room look for? What are the signs that teachers' words and actions foster the growth, development, and learning of toddlers? How will the visitor know that the toddlers are thriving in this setting? The supportive interactions teachers have with toddlers share the following characteristics.

* Most interactions take place at the children's level. Teachers sit on beanbag chairs, rocking chairs, and carpets where the children play. They invite toddlers to climb a ladder to the changing table, then establish eye contact while changing diapers and holding conversations. They sit with toddlers at snacktimes and mealtimes, using these routines as opportunities to get to know individuals and the group.

* Teachers use information provided by families to engage with children. A teacher might say, "Your mom told me that you can put on your shoes all by yourself. Do you want to show me?" Or a teacher might refer to a past or future event or connect it to a classroom event. "Your pop-pop told me that you went to the library this weekend. You borrowed a book about the blue truck—like the book we read on Friday."

* Teachers communicate that they appreciate and enjoy being in the company of toddlers. They celebrate progress and accomplishments and accept the predictable and unpredictable actions of toddlers. "You worked hard to build that tall tower. Then you knocked it down. Are you going to build it again?"

* Teachers know that toddlers receive and interpret messages from them all the time—through words, facial expressions, body language, and more. They make sure their communications are positive and enhance the overall well-being of toddlers.

But most of all, supportive interactions tell toddlers, "I like you. I see you growing and learning. I think you are amazing. You are an important member of our class, your family, and your community."

What Supportive Interactions Should Look Like

Caring for toddlers who are always on the move and somewhat unpredictable can be very demanding. In high-quality programs, teachers stay calm and encouraging. In the following examples, you will see what strategies and outcomes should be in place when you visit a toddler program and why these are important.

What you should see	Why
Teachers play with one or a few toddlers, modeling how to share, take turns, and use other social skills.	Toddlers are moving from solo play to play alongside other children. In time they will play with each other, using the same toys and materials. Modeling play skills allows toddlers to see them in use and practice using them too.
Teachers accommodate toddlers' desires to be independent and their need to stay close to familiar people and places.	Toddlers struggle to balance a strong desire to do things for themselves with their attachment to the familiar. They gain strength from checking in with adults before returning to their independent pursuits.
Teachers listen to, repeat, interpret, and respond to toddler communications.	Toddler communication is sometimes unclear, vague, and nonlinear. Active listening and rephrasing a toddler's words can contribute to understanding, allowing teachers to respond to and address a child's requests.
Toddlers show empathy and concern for their peers and ask an adult for help if needed.	Toddlers who attend child development programs have a lot of experience observing and building relationships with other children. They want their friends to be okay and know that adults can help a crying classmate or provide ice for a bumped knee.
Teachers and toddlers work together to clean up spills and messes using sponges, small brooms, and other cleanup tools.	Cleanup is fun for toddlers and allows them to express their desire to be independent. When toddlers and teachers work together, toddlers learn that it's okay when paint gets on the floor or when some applesauce gets on the table. They feel capable and in control as they help to clean up spills and messes.
Teachers and toddlers hold conversations about topics of interest to the children; teachers model how to keep a conversation going.	Conversations have guidelines such as waiting for a turn to speak or staying on topic when responding to a conversation partner. The most effective way to learn the rules is to take part in conversations with someone—in this case a teacher—who already knows how conversations work best.
Teachers help families and toddlers reunite at the end of the day.	Toddlers tend to be unpredictable; one day they are eager to see their parents at pickup time, and other days they cry because they want to stay and play with their classmates. A teacher might help by describing the child's day or sharing photos of an activity. The parent can now invite the child to talk about what she did. Or the teacher might have the child share something she made or a book they read.

What you should see	Why
Teachers learn and use a few important words and phrases in toddlers' home languages.	For young children, hearing their home language triggers feelings of warmth and security. They feel that there are connections between home and their program. Families also appreciate teachers' efforts to say a few words in their home language, especially the correct pronunciation of their names.
Teachers spend one-on-one time with each child at some time during the day.	Children who are quiet or who never seem to need a teacher's assistance can be easily overlooked. All children benefit from a teachers' individual attention, however. If the attention is thoughtful and honest, it does not have to take a lot of time. For example, one-on-one time could take place upon arrival, during a meal, at naptime, while getting ready to go outside, or at any other time when the teacher and child have an opportunity to engage in a meaningful way.
Teachers encourage toddlers' development of new skills by responding to each child's requests and cues as to whether support is desired.	Toddler development is uneven from child to child and within each child. Some can put on their socks; others need assistance. A child could have strong verbal skills but lack the confidence needed to achieve a physical goal such as climbing to the top of the slide. Teachers need to pay attention and provide what is needed, tailored to fit the child's unique personality and skill levels.
Teachers use caring language, tone of voice, and physical touch to let toddlers know they are appreciated and valued.	Toddlers thrive when they have warm relationships with the important adults in their lives. They look to adults for security, guidance, and support and enjoy sitting beside or in the lap of a caring teacher.
Teachers congratulate toddlers on progress as well as achievement of goals and observe to see when the child is interested in pursuing a new goal.	Learning something new can take a long time and receiving acknowledgment for progress made is a great motivator. Upon achievement of a goal, children need time to practice their new skill before moving on to the next step. For example, toddlers who learn to propel a riding toy with their feet do not need to move on to a tricycle. They can enjoy and practice their new skill as long as it holds interest.

When Interactions Need Further Adjusting

For deeper insight into the effectiveness of the supportive interactions between teachers and toddlers, observing in the classroom is important. If you spot warning signs such as those in the examples described below, it's time to look more closely and try to identify what might be causing the situation. Discuss the possible solutions noted in the third column with teachers and help them better understand how supportive interactions nurture and foster the development of toddlers.

Note: Some of the warning signs listed below may be caused by factors other than nonsupportive interactions or by a combination of nonsupportive interactions and other factors. Regular observations will provide information about the precise cause of the problem.

Warning sign	Why this might be happening	How educators can address the problem
Teachers laugh at toddlers whose efforts to do something on their own are not immediately and completely successful.	Teachers see the imperfect outcome of the child's efforts instead of the progress the child is making. Also, teachers find it humorous and spontaneously burst out in laughter, not realizing they may be hurting the child's feelings. For example, it is amusing when Jackson wears his underpants backward so he can see the decoration. However, his teacher should congratulate Jackson for independently putting on his underpants and using the toilet.	Lead teachers in recalling what took place when they were learning to do something new. What did they do first? How did they feel when their efforts were not completely successful? What did other people say and do? What was helpful and what was not? Then discuss the steps toddlers go through when learning to do things on their own. Ask what teaching behaviors are supportive and which are unintentionally disrespectful.
Teachers raise their voices as they argue or are unpleasant to each other within toddlers' earshot.	Teachers may feel frustrated and are taking it out on each other. They may need to learn some stress management techniques. They probably think that the toddlers do not notice what they are doing.	Visit the classroom several times at different times of the day. Try to identify what might be causing teachers to be stressed. Then meet with teachers to figure out how to reduce or remove the stressors. Remind teachers that toddlers learn from everything they see and hear and are frightened by raised voices.
Teachers interact with toddlers primarily to give directions or to reprimand a child for misbehaving. Mealtimes, for example, are spent telling toddlers what and how to eat instead of sharing interests and experiences.	Teachers may not know how to converse with toddlers; they may feel silly talking to a two-year-old. They may not realize that a toddler's day should include many positive interactions and exchanges.	Ask teachers to use a simple method to keep track of their interactions with toddlers. For example, they might start the day with a pocketful of counting bears and move a bear to the other pocket each time they have a conversation with a toddler. After an initial assessment of how often they engage with toddlers, they might set goals for the day and track progress in the same way.

Warning sign	Why this might be happening	How educators can address the problem
Teachers ignore or reject family requests and suggestions about supporting their toddler's achievement of goals—such as toilet learning.	Teachers may think they know best because they spend their days with toddlers. They may believe that families are not as well informed or skilled as they are, especially when there are cultural differences regarding developmental milestones. Teachers may not appreciate that families are the experts when it comes to their own child.	Suggest that family-teacher progress meetings include a planning strategy for goals that are likely to come up before the next conference. Ask several teachers to work together to create a format for discussing and setting joint goals. Remind teachers that while they do know a lot about toddlers, families know about their child's whole life, from birth on.
Teachers do things for toddlers that the toddlers could do on their own.	Teachers may come from a culture in which toddlers are not encouraged to be independent. Instead, adults show their love and caring by doing things for children at this age. Or teachers may think it is faster, tidier, and more efficient just to do things themselves.	Lead a workshop focused on toddler independence. One activity can be to consider a particular task—for example, getting ready to go outdoors—and determine what toddlers can do on their own and where they really do need adult assistance. For example, toddlers can get their sun hats from their cubbies, and teachers can apply sunscreen.
Teachers tell toddlers they are too old to do something, such as use a pacifier, cry, wet their pants, or spill a cup of milk.	Teachers may truly believe that toddlers are too old for a certain behavior or worry that the behavior may continue into the preschool and school-age years. They may think the child will be spoiled if they allow the behavior to continue.	Offer a variety of print and digital resources to help teachers review typical toddler development, underscoring that each child has a unique timetable for development. Explain that respecting and responding to a child's stage of development and needs will never cause a child to be spoiled. Discuss appropriate ways to respond to these behaviors that address the child's needs.
Teachers ignore or delay responding to a toddler's request, for no apparent reason.	Teachers may not be paying attention to the children, so they do not notice the request. Or perhaps the teacher is busy and doesn't realize that acknowledging the request will help the toddler handle the wait time until the teacher is available.	When you witness a behavior such as this, wait before drawing a conclusion about the reason for the teacher's lack of a response. Meet with the teacher to describe what you saw and heard. Ask the teacher what he or she was thinking at the time and what she thinks the toddler needed.
Teachers take over children's play, telling them what to do and how to use materials. "No, do it like this."	Teachers may think they are being helpful because the toddlers are doing it wrong or will have more fun and greater success if they follow their directions.	Invite the teacher to co-observe a group of toddlers at play. Compare your notes and use them as a way to start a discussion about the role of teachers in supporting, but not directing, toddlers' play.

Positive Guidance

In a high-quality toddler program, the teachers support development and learning, including learning what behaviors are acceptable and how to manage and express strong feelings. The teachers have appropriate expectations for toddlers and set limits that keep the children safe while allowing them to continue to strive for independence. Through positive guidance, teachers acknowledge and accept toddlers' feelings, while helping children recognize and name those emotions and learn how to express them in words.

Self-regulation—the ability to control bodily functions, manage powerful emotions, maintain focus and attention, and delay gratification—is an important goal during the early childhood years. Positive guidance helps toddlers make progress in learning to control impulses and do what is necessary, even when it is not what they want to do. Teachers help toddlers learn how to wait for a turn, state what they want to do, ask for a toy, and know when it's time to take a break.

Foundations Underlying Quality

How might a visitor to a toddler classroom recognize the use of positive guidance strategies that help children learn how to regulate their behavior? What are the signs that children are learning to recognize, name, and manage strong feelings? Positive guidance for toddlers reflects the following beliefs and actions:

☀ Toddlers are at their own unique stage of development. They are neither a bigger version of infants nor a smaller version of preschoolers. They are active learners whose skills are expanding in all areas of development.

☀ Toddlers are at a developmental stage where they are egocentric, meaning they are largely focused on themselves. They do not understand how other people feel and don't recognize how their actions affect others. Calm, understanding teachers can gently nudge them through this stage.

☀ Toddlers can and will learn from positive guidance strategies. They want to please adults and enjoy being with other children.

☀ Toddlers thrive on consistency. It is important for teachers and families to work together, creating and applying positive guidance at home and at the program.

What Positive Guidance Should Look Like

In a toddler room, teachers use a variety of individualized positive guidance strategies to prevent unsafe behaviors and foster development and learning. They calmly remind children of rules and guidelines, redirect them to alternative activities, offer choices, and accept the unique characteristics of this age group. In the following examples, you will see what strategies and outcomes should be in place when you visit a toddler program and why these are important.

What you should see	Why
The environment is designed to support toddlers' active play and explorations while also ensuring that teachers and families are comfortable.	Creating an environment that reflects current stages of toddler development, cultures, home languages, families, and interests will prevent most problem behaviors.
Teachers use positive statements to tell children what to do rather than what not to do. For example, "Walk indoors," "Hold your cup with two hands," "Jump on the pillows," and "Get the other firefighter hat from the shelf."	Toddlers are more likely to learn from being told what to do rather than what not to do. They hear and understand positive requests immediately. Telling the child what not to do does not explain what behavior is okay.
Teachers involve the toddlers in setting a few simple rules, phrased in positive terms.	Toddlers are more likely to understand and follow rules they helped set. They can remember a few rules, such as "Be nice to each other" and "Take care of our toys." Learning to follow a few rules helps toddlers become self-regulated.
Teachers privately congratulate toddlers when they remember to follow the rules.	Toddlers can be embarrassed by public congratulations, so a one-on-one conversation is a more effective way to reinforce a positive behavior. For example, "I saw you hand the last block to William so he could finish his tower. You were nice to William."
Teachers review with toddlers the procedures for a walk in the neighborhood, field trip, or other new experience.	Toddlers feel more secure when they know what is going to happen and in what order. Security supports positive behavior, so there are less likely to be problems when toddlers know what to expect.
Teachers gently hold and acknowledge the feelings of a toddler who has lost control or is having a tantrum; they help to calm the child before making any suggestions. For example, "I can see you are frustrated. You wanted to finish the puzzle, but Angela knocked it over. It's upsetting when your plans have to change."	Toddlers can feel scared and uncertain when they lose control. They need a teacher to acknowledge and allow them to express their feelings as long as their outburst is not hurting themselves or anyone else. A teacher's calm response helps the child to calm himself.
Teachers offer acceptable alternatives to address toddlers' needs or respond to their requests. For example, "The fire trucks are all in use now. You can use this truck or this car."	Toddlers feel a sense of control and independence when they can choose—from alternatives that adults find acceptable. This strategy works in most situations that arise in the toddler years. For example, "You can have an apple or a banana." "Would you like to read this book or this one?" "Do you want to put the blue shirt or the striped shirt on the doll?"

What you should see	Why
Teachers use books and stories about typical experiences and challenges told through puppets, stuffed animals, and dolls to help toddlers learn to recognize, name, and manage strong feelings.	Toddlers tend to have strong feelings. They may be elated about one thing and angry about another. Learning to manage and express feelings in words begins with being able to recognize and name feelings—their own and those of other children. They learn the names for emotions from teachers while reading and discussing books about feelings, and they practice naming and expressing feelings using toys such as puppets, dolls, and stuffed animals.
Teachers give children time to resolve their differences; if the disagreement goes on too long, they step in to offer to help. For example, "I think you both got to the slide at the same time. How can you decide who will go first?"	Toddlers are learning to get along with each other, and part of that process is figuring out how to resolve disagreements. Often they can problem solve on their own. Allowing them time to work out a problem communicates respect. For example, "I know you can figure this out by yourselves." If it looks as though the children are unable to solve the disagreement, teachers can ask them if they would like some help.
Teachers include opportunities for toddlers to say no while reading books, singing songs, doing fingerplays, and asking silly questions.	Toddlers feel in control when they say no. That's why this age group is known for saying no to any request. Because toddlers have acquired so much information, it's easy to give them a chance to say no in a positive way. For example, teachers can ask, "Do ducks live in trees?" or "Can you reach the sky?" By saying no as part of a story or activity, toddlers get to feel a sense of control while having fun.
Teachers provide tools, materials, time, and encouragement so toddlers can experience success.	Toddlers enjoy learning new things, but it can be frustrating when it takes longer than anticipated to gain a new skill. Teachers can help by making sure the conditions for success are in place. For example, if a toddler needs more time and a spoon to eat her peas, then both can be provided.
Teachers have appropriate expectations for toddlers; they provide specific instructions for carrying out a request.	Many experiences are new to toddlers. They may not know what a teacher's brief request means. For example, "Clean up" is more readily understandable to an older child or adult. Toddlers are more likely to comply with a more specific request, such as, "Put the toys back on the shelf" or "Hang up your coat on the hook underneath your photograph."

When the twelve items noted above are in place, the positive guidance strategies in your program are likely to support toddlers' growth, development, and learning. Use the checklist in appendix C to observe how well your program meets these criteria. For items that your program is not yet addressing well, work with teachers to devise and implement an action plan for improvement. As a supervisor, you are responsible for ensuring that positive guidance strategies are optimally serving children and teachers.

When Guidance Strategies Need Further Adjusting

For deeper insight into the effectiveness of the program's positive guidance approach, it's important to observe toddlers and their teachers. Knowledge of positive guidance strategies does not always translate into their effective use. If you spot warning signs such as those in the examples described below, it's time to look more closely and try to identify what might be causing the situation. Discuss the possible solutions noted in the third column with teachers and help them better understand how positive guidance is a teaching strategy that helps children learn how to behave in acceptable ways.

Note: Some of the warning signs listed below may be caused by factors other than inappropriate guidance strategies or by a combination of inappropriate guidance strategies and other factors. Regular observations will provide information about the precise cause of the problem.

Warning sign	Why this might be happening	How educators can address the problem
Teachers frequently remind toddlers of the class rules and limits.	There may be too many rules for toddlers to remember, or the rules may be stated in negative terms so toddlers don't know what to do. Teachers may have unrealistic expectations for toddlers' behavior.	Help teachers make a list of all the rules toddlers are expected to follow, indoors and outdoors. Discuss the reason for each rule and decide which ones are necessary. Combine rules that are redundant and eliminate rules that have no purpose. Guide teachers in writing rules using positive language.
Teachers repeatedly say no throughout the day.	There are many reasons teachers might say no so often. The curriculum, environment, or expectations could be inappropriate for the age or for this group of toddlers. Perhaps teachers do not know positive guidance strategies that prevent problems and support self-regulation.	Provide a supply of pennies and have teachers put a penny in a jar—on a high shelf out of toddlers' reach—each time they hear themselves say no. This should result in an awareness of the problem. The next step is for teachers to review their program to identify what might be causing them to repeatedly tell children to stop what they are doing.

Warning sign	Why this might be happening	How educators can address the problem
Teachers lose their tempers and raise their voices when reprimanding toddlers.	Stress, caused by the job or other circumstances, can overwhelm some teachers, especially teachers who lack the knowledge and skills needed to guide toddlers' behavior.	Intervene as quickly as possible so the teacher can regain composure and control. In a private meeting, explain that this behavior is always inappropriate. It scares toddlers and does nothing to help them learn positive behaviors. Offer to help the teacher gain the knowledge and skills needed for the job. If the teacher's performance does not improve, it may be necessary to suggest that this individual pursue another career.
Teachers respond to a toddler's aggressive behavior with aggression. For example, when a toddler kicks a teacher, the teacher kicks the toddler back.	A teacher may respond in this way because he or she thinks that the child needs to "learn how it feels to be kicked." This could be a guidance approach used in the teacher's family. Or it could be an automatic response, unchecked by self-control.	Intervene as quickly as possible so the teacher does not continue to use this approach. Explain that what toddlers learn from this kind of guidance is that adults—who are bigger and stronger than children—cannot be trusted. They do not learn to control their own urges or to use their words to express their feelings. Again, offer to help the teacher gain the knowledge and skills needed for the job, including the ability to control one's own reactions. If the teacher's performance does not improve, it may be necessary to suggest that this individual pursue another career.
Teachers tease and make fun of toddlers who have not learned to use the toilet, drink from a cup, or dress themselves.	Teachers may think that teasing and mocking are strategies that will encourage children to gain self-help skills. They may think their job will be easier, or toddlers will learn more if all of them are toilet trained and use self-help skills.	Explain to teachers why teasing and mocking cause more harm than good and are not appropriate ways to encourage toddler development. Review child development principles, such as children follow individual timetables for development. Discuss why it is not helpful to push children to learn something they are not yet ready to learn.
Teachers punish toddlers who act out or neglect to follow directions.	Teachers may think that punishment is effective, not realizing that it does not help toddlers progress toward self-regulation. They may be frustrated because they do not know of any other way to "make" toddlers behave. Or they may not have the background needed to understand toddler behavior. Perhaps parents have requested that the teacher punish their child.	Acknowledge that being a toddler teacher is a tough job. However, toddler teachers will find it more enjoyable and rewarding if they learn more about this age group—what they are like, what they can and cannot do, and how to guide them in positive ways. Also, remind teachers that punishment is not permitted in your program.

Warning sign	Why this might be happening	How educators can address the problem
Teachers yell at or isolate toddlers who are in the middle of a tantrum.	Teachers may believe that toddlers can control their tantrums—stop them at will and in response to an adult's request. They may think that ignoring or isolating the child will teach the child to stop having tantrums.	Lead a workshop on the biological causes of tantrums—the still developing prefrontal cortex that governs self-regulation of emotions and other behaviors. Suggest observing to learn what might trigger a certain child to have a tantrum—what makes the child go from anger and frustration to a loss of control. Also, address the possible purpose of the tantrum and how the adult's response should match the purpose. Suggest eliminating the trigger or anticipating the toddler's likely response. For example, if a teacher realizes that a child has a tantrum when hungry, then she needs an early snack. Or if a tantrum is likely inevitable, the teacher can be ready to respond appropriately.
Teachers keep the toddlers in one large group all day; by the end of the day, some toddlers are trying to get away from the group while others are crying and acting out.	Teachers may think this is an appropriate way to lead a toddler class. Perhaps they think they are preparing toddlers for school. Or they may find it easier to keep track of the children if they are all together.	Plan a visit to an effective and well-arranged toddler classroom that can serve as a model for your program's teachers. Observe how teachers engage children and how children use the environment. Help teachers arrange their classrooms with several learning centers, an open area for movement and meetings, and a few "be by myself" spaces where toddlers can get away from the group. Have teachers keep track of toddlers' behavior and engagement before and after the room rearrangement.

4 Ensuring the Effectiveness of Preschool Programs

When entering a preschool classroom, you want to observe a hub of activity and learning taking place. Children this age are curious and inquisitive and eager to discover how the world around them works. They benefit most from being in a program where they can independently participate in activities of their own choosing and explore and experiment with materials in depth. The teacher's role in a preschool classroom is to facilitate and guide children's learning by providing both child-initiated learning and direct instruction as needed.

You can use the information and guidance in this chapter to oversee the program environment, toys, materials and equipment, program structure, curriculum, supportive interactions, and positive guidance. When all these features are in place and working as they should, children ages three to five are primed to develop and learn to their full potential.

This chapter includes the following sections:

☀ Environment, pages 98–104

☀ Toys, Materials, and Equipment, pages 105–113

☀ Program Structure, pages 114–120

☀ Curriculum: Activities and Experiences, pages 121–127

☀ Supportive Interactions, pages 128–133

☀ Positive Guidance, pages 134–139

Environment

The starting point for overseeing and maintaining high-quality preschool programming is the physical environment. How the program's space is laid out and designed provides the underpinning for all teaching and learning. Indeed, the program design is a blueprint for curriculum implementation. It also creates a physical and social atmosphere that reflects your program's philosophy and enables teachers to support individual and group progress.

Foundations Underlying Quality

Before observing the effectiveness of the program environment, you will need to be sure certain baseline standards for quality are being met. These standards include the size of the indoor and outdoor settings, health and safety measures, and how the setting is arranged to support children and teachers.

Program Space

Preschool programs are housed in a wide variety of dedicated or adapted spaces, ranging from school and center classrooms to trailers to church basements. Standards for indoor space are set by federal (in the case of Head Start, military child development, and Department of Defense Education Activity [DoDEA] programs), state, local, and tribal licensing authorities and will vary, so you need to check your own licensing agency for governing requirements on square footage. Head Start programs, for example, have to comply with state, tribal, or local licensing regulations but must provide a minimum of thirty-five square feet per child, exclusive of space for toileting, storage, and built-in furnishings (Office of Head Start 2017).

Because the amount of space directly correlates with quality, exceeding these requirements will benefit children. *Caring for Our Children*, a compilation of health and safety performance standards issued jointly by the American Academy of Pediatrics, the American Public Health Association, and the National Resource Center for Health and Safety in Child Care and Early Education notes that "historically, a standard of thirty-five square feet was used. Recommendations from research studies range between forty-two to fifty-four square feet per child. Child behavior tends to be more constructive when sufficient space is organized to promote developmentally appropriate skills. Crowding has been shown to be associated with increased risk of developing upper respiratory infections. Also, having sufficient space will reduce the risk of injury from simultaneous activities" (American Academy of Pediatrics 2011, 203). *Caring for Our Children* recommends a minimum of forty-two square feet per child, excluding storage, major pieces of equipment, and built-in furnishings, but fifty square feet of usable floor space is "preferred" (American Academy of Pediatrics 2011).

The space designated for outdoor play and learning may be adjacent to the classroom, a short walk away, or on a fenced-in rooftop. The outdoor area includes soil, sand, grass, hills, and flat, hard surfaces. If there is no suitable play area within walking distance of the program, gross-motor play can take place in a gym or activity room. This latter setup should be supplemented with frequent outdoor walks and field trips so children can benefit from being outdoors daily.

While federal, state, local, and tribal regulations may vary, both the Head Start Program Performance Standards and *Caring for Our Children* require that there be seventy-five square feet of space per preschool child for children playing outdoors or in an indoor gym / activity room (American Academy of Pediatrics 2011). Other resources extend the recommendation to 100 square feet per child (Click, Karkos, and Robertson 2013).

Health and Safety

Before supervisors can effectively monitor how the environment supports children and teachers, the setting must be checked to ensure it is safe and healthy for children. Your local, state, or tribal licensing agency issues mandatory health and safety guidelines. Head Start and military child development / Sure Start programs have stringent standards for health and safety requirements.

To ensure that your program's environment complies with indoor and outdoor health and safety requirements, we have included a checklist in appendix A. Though not all-inclusive, this checklist reflects Head Start and military child development / Sure Start program requirements. Once you are assured that children are safe and healthy, you can concentrate on how the environment facilitates the growth, development, and learning of preschoolers.

Room / Outdoor Space Arrangement

Best practices in the preschool years include arranging the indoor setting into distinct learning centers where children can explore and experiment with materials by themselves, in pairs with a friend, or in small or large groups. This arrangement allows teachers to observe, interact with, and support young children's learning.

While there will be variation across programs, a well-planned and supportive setting for preschoolers includes these learning centers:

- ❈ **Blocks**: Protected on three sides and located adjacent to dramatic play so children's play can spill over from one center to the other. Children construct block buildings, roads, towers, and other structures.

- ❈ **Dramatic play**: Includes a home area with child-size appliances and toy foods for cooking and serving. Dress-up clothes and other props allow children to pretend and re-create familiar experiences.

- ❈ **Art**: Located near a sink, the center includes child-size tables and chairs and two-sided easels. Children paint, draw, make collages, and sculpt using playdough, clay, and other modeling materials.

- ❈ **Literacy**: Located in a quiet area away from noisy play. Includes book display shelves, child-size table and chairs, and beanbag chairs and other comfortable seating. Children look at books and other texts, use computers, write, and make books.

- **Music and movement**: In a large, carpeted area, children listen to music, make musical instruments, dance, do yoga and movement activities, and march with musical instruments.

- **Science (discovery)**: Located near a window or light source with a nearby child-size table, children explore natural items, conduct experiments, and make charts of their results. They also grow plants and care for pets.

- **Math and manipulatives**: Located in a carpeted area with child-size table and chairs. Children complete puzzles, play board games, and build with Lego blocks and other small building materials.

- **Sand play / water play**: Located near a water source in a space with washable flooring. Includes sand/water tables or large tubs. Children play, experiment, and explore science and math concepts.

- **Cooking**: Located near a sink and electrical outlets with a child-size table and chairs. Children serve themselves snacks, follow recipe cards, and take part in cooking activities.

In addition, the preschool setting includes the following:

- a family greeting space where family members sign in and teachers communicate and exchange information with families about each child's daily routines and activities at home and at the program

- cubbies for storing personal items from home

- spaces where children can get away from group activities and be by themselves (in view of teachers)

- locked storage areas for adult belongings

- an area for storing cots or mats used at naptime

- a bathroom with child-size sinks and toilets (in the room or in a nearby hallway)

The outdoor space is also divided into defined areas, although these areas do not need to be defined with visible boundaries in the same way that indoor learning centers do. Suggested outdoor areas include spaces where children can engage in the following activities:

- ride trikes and other wheeled toys
- pull and push wagons and wheelbarrows
- climb, swing, and slide
- create and build with loose parts
- throw, catch, and kick balls
- experiment with sand and water
- make music

- play games
- look at books
- engage in pretend play
- do woodworking
- draw, paint, and write
- garden
- care for animals

What the Environment Should Look Like

Preschool children flourish in a well-organized, clearly defined environment that is arranged to promote independence, foster decision making, and encourage initiative and involvement. Such an environment also supports social and emotional learning and allows children to make friends, enjoy each other's company, and identify, express, and cope with strong emotions in appropriate ways. An effective preschool classroom is divided into attractive and inviting learning centers that offer children a range of activity choices that reflect their ever-changing interests and support all children's learning and development. Areas are set up so children can choose to work and play alone, with a friend, or as part of a small group.

In a well-planned environment, children can achieve goals set by educators in conjunction with the children's families. Listed below are examples of what you should see in a center-based program serving preschoolers and why these arrangements of the environment are important.

What you should see	Why
A family bulletin board / message center with current news about the program, photos of the children's activities, and samples of children's creations.	Families are eager to know what their child does and learns at the program. Welcoming families to the program invites them to partner with teachers on behalf of children.
Photographs of the children are prominently displayed in their cubbies and throughout the classroom. Photos of the children with their families are posted in the classroom and in "All about Me" books in the literacy center.	When children see photographs of themselves and their families, they develop a sense of belonging. Family photos enable children to "keep in touch" with their families during the day. Such photos also show appreciation for diversity. Photographs taken at the program allow children to revisit and discuss their experiences.
Furnishings (such as low shelving, dividers, bookcases, two-sided easels, child-size tables), flooring textures, tape, and exits clearly define centers and manage traffic flow.	Creative use of exits, furnishings, flooring, and tape draws children into centers and minimizes running. Such arrangements allow children to become involved in their play without being distracted by activities elsewhere in the room.
Noisy centers are separated from quiet ones. For example, the blocks and dramatic play centers are located near each other, away from the more quiet literacy and math and manipulatives centers.	Noisy, active play is appropriate and even essential in some centers. In other centers where children focus on quiet tasks, it's best to have fewer distractions.
Messy activities like cooking, art, and sand/water play take place on washable flooring, while blocks, dramatic play, science, music, math and manipulatives, and literacy take place on carpeted floors.	Children need to be free to create with abandon. Having washable flooring allows them to be creatively messy during art, cooking, and sand and water play. Carpeting in areas that are not likely to be messy zones allows preschoolers to be comfortable sitting on the floor doing a puzzle or looking at a book.

What you should see	Why
Quiet "be by myself" spaces such as nooks and lofts with soft seating where children can work/play alone or with a friend.	Children who spend long hours in a group need cozy places to relax, de-stress, and get away from noise and activity. Being able to recoup their energy contributes to children's well-being and helps them build self-regulation.
Spaces accommodate several children playing together. For example, there is space for children to play a board game, paint a mural, or put on a play.	Learning centers need to be large enough for a small group of children to engage in cooperative play and develop social skills. When there is plenty of space to carry out their plans, children are less likely to have disagreements.
Materials are displayed on low shelving labeled with pictures and words (in both English and the children's home languages).	Labels allow children to make choices as they independently select materials and return them when finished. When children know where things belong, they can help to maintain a neat, organized environment. Labeling also supports emerging literacy.
Print appears in all of the home languages of the children and in English. When multiple home languages are present, signage is color coded to signify particular home languages. For example, blue text could mean Spanish and red Arabic.	Featuring home languages throughout the environment demonstrates respect for the unique characteristics of each child. Children are more likely to feel comfortable and ready to learn when they feel a sense of belonging.
Children's art, creations, and writing samples are prominently displayed at the children's eye level (not higher than four and a half feet from the floor) on classroom walls. Commercial displays are limited.	Children feel proud to see their work displayed. They can revisit their creations and recall what they did. They can also share and discuss their work with their families and other visitors.
Materials and displays represent the children's home lives. For example, books, dolls, wooden people props, dress-up clothes, music, food props, and real foods served at snack and in cooking activities reflect each child's culture and family structure.	Children feel included and valued when they see familiar images and items found in their homes at the program; these items remind them of their families. They are more likely to participate in activities and engage in learning when they are made to feel that their family's background is welcomed and respected at the program.
Landscape features are used in the layout of the outdoor space. Plants, bushes, trees, and gardens are incorporated into the design.	Placing a basket of books in a shaded area or using a tree stump as a woodworking bench makes nature part of the learning setting. Natural boundaries like bushes or a shallow creek can define activity spaces.

When the twelve items noted above are in place, the environment is likely to support the growth, development, and learning of preschoolers. Use the checklist in appendix D to observe how well your program meets these criteria. For items that your program is not yet addressing well, work with teachers to devise and implement an action plan for improvement. As a supervisor, you are responsible for ensuring that all components of the indoor and outdoor environment are optimally serving children and teachers.

When the Environment Needs Further Adjusting

For deeper insight into the effectiveness of the environment, it's important to observe how children use the indoor and outdoor spaces. It's one thing to have a well-designed and laid out environment. However, unless children are using it as planned, it will not serve the program well. If you spot children engaged in behaviors such as those described below, the environment may be contributing to problems that hamper their progress. Discuss the possible solutions noted in the third column with teachers and help them implement these countermeasures, if appropriate.

Note: Some of the warning signs listed below may be caused by factors other than the environment or by a combination of environmental and nonenvironmental factors. Regular observations will provide information about the cause of the problem.

Warning sign	Why this might be happening	How educators can address the problem
Children run throughout the space.	Pathways are not clearly defined or are too wide. Learning centers are set up around a central path, which acts like a runway. Furnishings are pushed against the wall, creating open spaces that invite running.	Work with teachers to review the layout of pathways and adjust them as needed. Try setting up centers in a zigzag pattern to eliminate a large central area. Move the entrances to learning centers as needed to redirect traffic.
Children yell to each other from across the room.	Pathways may be blocked or overly complicated. As a result, children may yell to get a friend's attention rather than seeking out that child.	Encourage teachers to walk the pathways as children would do to identify obstacles and furnishings that are difficult to get around. Have teachers remove or rearrange items to improve the traffic flow.
Children wander around unengaged or do the same activities over and over.	Children can't see or reach all of the play options available to them. They use only what is easily accessible.	Review with teachers how materials are displayed. Make sure every toy, material, and piece of equipment is placed so that children can quickly identify what it is, take it out, and return it independently.

Warning sign	Why this might be happening	How educators can address the problem
Children leave an area before finishing a task or completing an activity.	The area may be so open that children are distracted by others and by activities taking place elsewhere. Or noisy centers may be too close to quiet activities.	Brainstorm with teachers how to reconfigure the centers to make them more protected. Move the noisy centers farther away from quiet ones.
Children bump into one another, interrupt one another's play, and unintentionally knock over one another's creations.	Too many children are using the centers at one time. Or the centers are not well defined and children walk through them to move about the classroom.	Have teachers set up a system for identifying the maximum number of children who can play in a center at one time. They could limit the number of painting smocks, chairs at a table, or lanyards hanging on a hook at the entrance. If centers need better definition, rearrange divider shelves and other furnishings. Mark boundaries by applying tape to the floor.
Children crawl or hide under tables.	Children want to get away from the group, and there are no nooks or lofts where they can be alone. Or tables are grouped together or not housed in centers where they contribute to play.	Together with teachers, scout the room to find places where children can be alone. Make sure there are cozy pillows, beanbag chairs, or other soft seating where children can be by themselves. Make sure that tables and chairs are integrated into learning centers where they contribute to play (for example, art, literacy, cooking, and math and manipulatives) and not congregated in a common area.
Children leave out their playthings when they are done using them.	The environment is so messy that cleaning seems overwhelming and children do not know how to start. Or the storage areas are poorly labeled so children don't know where to return materials when they are done using them.	Ask teachers to take a fresh look at how materials are displayed in each center. Make sure that items are not crowded and that labels with pictures and words clearly identify storage areas. Consider ways to enhance the shelving and the centers so children will be able to help maintain a neat, orderly environment.

Toys, Materials, and Equipment

The effectiveness of well-designed indoor and outdoor environments is directly dependent on how these areas are stocked with equipment, toys, and materials. High-quality preschool programs contain a rich and varied supply of toys, materials, and equipment appropriate for the ages, stages, abilities, cultures, languages, and other characteristics of the children in the group. They both match and challenge the children's wide range of skills and knowledge. Children need to experience success and, at the same time, to be sufficiently challenged to learn new skills and concepts.

Foundations Underlying Quality

Before observing the equipment, toys, and materials in your program's indoor and outdoor environments to ensure their effectiveness, you will need to be sure that certain baseline standards for quality are being met. These standards include the developmental appropriateness of your inventory and their adherence to safety.

Selection of Toys, Materials, and Equipment

A high-quality preschool program is stocked with toys and materials that encourage children's creativity, problem solving, exploration, experimentation, and learning in all areas of development. In addition, because the environment is divided into learning centers, the toys, materials, and equipment need to address the experiences and activities that take place in each learning center. For example, the inventory in the art center needs to facilitate children's visual explorations and art creations—drawing, painting, sculpting, molding, weaving, cutting and pasting, and woodworking.

Because every program, and the children and families served, has unique characteristics, no one master inventory is appropriate for all preschool classrooms. Your selections should reflect the interests, experiences, backgrounds, and cultures of the children in the group, as well as your budget. In addition, if children in your program have special needs, the inventory needs to be supplemented with toys, materials, and equipment that are adapted so all children can fully participate in the program.

The following lists are in no way exhaustive. Rather, these lists are a starting point for checking that your program has an age-appropriate, individually appropriate, and culturally appropriate inventory for preschoolers (Dodge et al. 2016).

Blocks center

* set of hardwood unit blocks (approximately 390 pieces)
* set of hollow blocks (approximately 48 pieces)
* cardboard blocks
* large plastic blocks
* foam blocks
* PVC pipes and connectors
* ramps
* wooden people props of both genders and varying ethnicities
* wooden animal props
* wooden transportation props (traffic signs, train set, cars, buses, fire trucks, airplanes)
* wooden trees and other landscaping props
* child-size hard hats
* blueprint paper, writing tools, and clipboards
* picture books on construction

Art center

* freestanding, child-size double- or triple-sided easels
* child-size table with four to six chairs
* smocks
* drying rack
* chalkboards, chalk, and erasers
* whiteboard with dry-erase markers
* markers and jumbo crayons
* pencils and gel pens
* stamp pads and stamps
* manila papers or newsprint for drawing and painting
* glazed papers or cafeteria trays for fingerpainting
* assorted papers (construction, tissue, crepe, butcher, and onionskin)
* assorted paintbrushes and paints
* alternative painting tools (toothbrushes, sponges, squirt bottles, and rollers)

* doughs/clays and props (hammers, rolling pins, and cookie cutters)
* papier-mâché and plaster of paris
* collage materials, including feathers, shells, cotton balls, leaves, flowers, netting, bottle caps, and buttons
* assorted materials for assemblages such as rubber bands, paper clips, wire, tape, pipe cleaners, twine, and clothespins
* child-size tools, such as safety scissors, hole punch, stapler, and staples
* glue, glue sticks, paste, and tape
* wire and dowels
* yarn and looms
* workbench with vise/C-clamp
* real tools for woodworking (nails, hammers, saws, and hand drills)
* pieces of soft wood and leather scraps
* safety goggles
* picture books on artists, art techniques, and color and design

Literacy center

Furniture

* beanbag chair, child-size rockers, or large pillows
* child-size table with two to four chairs for writing

Reading

* variety of picture books, big books, and early readers (as appropriate) featuring stories, fantasies, poetry, alphabet, counting, concepts, and predictable refrains
* variety of nonfiction books about topics of interest to children and to be used as references
* magazines for children
* bookstands for displaying books with the front cover facing out
* stand for holding big books
* MP3 player, CD player, tablet, or other digital devices with multiple headsets that are loaded with stories

Computer

- child-size computer stand/table with two chairs
- power surge protector
- desktop computer/printer/scanner/camera

ABCs, writing, and publishing

- assorted writing papers, lined and unlined
- assorted writing tools, such as markers, pencils, and crayons
- pencil sharpener
- alphabet stamps and stamp pad
- letter and number stencils
- ready-made blank books
- publishing tools, such as ruler, hole punch, safety scissors, stapler and staples, glue sticks, and yarn/shoelaces
- chalkboard and chalk
- clipboards / lap pads
- magnetic board and letters
- magic slates
- alphabet strips
- individual mailboxes for each child

Storytelling

- puppets
- puppet stage
- story clothesline (children use clothespins to hang pictures of story in sequence)
- storytelling apron (for teachers or children)
- flannel board and pieces
- hats and costumes related to books

DRAMATIC PLAY CENTER

- child-size kitchen furnishings, such as a table with four chairs, refrigerator, stove, microwave, and sink
- child-size lounge chair
- child-size ironing board and iron
- full-length mirror (shatter-proof, freestanding or attached to wall)

- plastic foods common to cultures of children in program
- child-size pots, pans, and cooking utensils
- child-size broom, dustpan, and mop
- decorations for kitchen/living area, such as curtains, tablecloths, plants, artwork, and other culturally relevant items
- props for use in scenarios—magazines, books, paper, pens, smartphones (old and pretend), calendars
- dolls of both genders and various ethnicities
- doll-size furniture, such as doll bed/cradle, high chair, chest of drawers, baby stroller/carriage, and couch
- stuffed animals
- dress-up clothes for men and women and accessories such as jewelry, purses, briefcases, hats, and backpacks
- prop boxes for additional settings, such as a school, a grocery store, and the vet's office
- cartons and furnishings that can be used to set up other pretend play settings

MUSIC AND MOVEMENT CENTER

- CD player with CDs, MP3 player, tablet, or other form of digital music, multiple sets of headphones
- music representative of various genres, such as classical, children's songs, folk, jazz, pop, reggae, rock, and other styles representative of children's cultures
- culturally relevant rhythm instruments, such as tambourine, rhythm sticks, bell bracelets, maracas, shakers, kazoo, triangle, bells, and drums
- homemade instruments such as drums and maracas
- scarves/streamers
- picture books on composers, singing, and music

Science center

* table for displaying materials
* magnifying glass
* balance scale
* microscope or computer microscope attachment (if possible)
* magnets
* prisms
* natural collections, such as leaves, seeds, and shells
* sorting containers/trays
* sorting tools, such as tweezers, eyedroppers, and tongs
* ant farm and classroom pets (such as fish and hamsters) in aquarium/cage with food nearby in sealed containers
* paper and writing tools
* plants, seeds, and soil
* discovery trays with loose parts, shiny objects, and wind-up objects
* sensory tubs with oobleck, shaving cream, and ice with salt
* small appliances (without sharp parts or pieces small enough to be swallowed) to take apart and put together using screwdrivers
* safety goggles
* picture books on plants, animals, and natural phenomena

Math and manipulatives center

* child-size table with four to six chairs
* puzzles, ranging from four knobbed pieces up to sixty-plus pieces without knobs
* Lego blocks
* Cuisenaire rods
* table blocks
* dominoes
* felt boards
* beads and pegs
* sewing cards
* card and lotto games
* board games
* self-help skill frames
* nesting boxes and cups
* stacking rings
* three-dimensional shape sorters
* parquetry blocks
* geoboards
* tangrams
* magnetic numbers and board
* interlocking links/cubes
* collectibles, such as bottle caps, buttons, keys, and nuts and bolts
* books on numbers, math concepts, and Lego block constructions

Sand play / water play center

* tables/tubs/basins
* waterproof smocks
* sterilized play sand
* props, such as measuring cups, funnels, shovels, basters, squirt bottles, colanders, buckets, whisks, eggbeaters, straws, tubing, combs, fishnets, marbles, and waterwheels
* collectibles, such as shells, plastic insects, and sterilized bones
* sorting tools, such as tongs and tweezers
* magnifying glass
* food coloring and soap
* bubble solution
* mops and sponges for cleanup
* picture books on sand, beaches, oceans, water, and ice

Cooking center

* child-size table with two to four chairs
* laminated recipe cards (in rebus format) with pictures and words
* stove or electric frying pan/wok (to be used with close supervision)
* aprons

- bowls of various sizes
- measuring cups and spoons
- cutting board and real knives (to be used with close supervision)
- utensils such as wooden spoons, whisks, eggbeater, peeler, spatulas, tongs, funnel, and potato masher
- can opener and cooking shears (to be used with close supervision)
- kitchen timer
- cake pans, loaf pans, and saucepans
- blender and hand mixer (to be used with close supervision)
- pot holders, dish towels, and trivets
- pitchers
- place mats, dishes, glasses, and flatware
- children's recipe books and picture books that feature foods and family meals
- laminated recipe cards (made by staff or parent volunteers)

Outdoors

Gross-motor play

- swings, slides, and climber
- balance beams, ramps, and tunnels
- wheeled toys like tricycles, big wheels, scooters, and wagons
- safety helmets
- jump ropes
- hula hoops
- beanbags
- balls and bats (several sizes)
- parachute/streamers
- large boxes

Sand and water play

- sandbox area with sterilized play sand, shovels, buckets, spoons, bowls, gelatin molds, plastic bottles (cut in half), funnels, and so on
- water table or a plastic basin; pails, buckets, and other props; and large house-painting brushes for painting buildings with water

Woodworking (to be done with close supervision)

- sawhorses
- boards and wood scraps
- real woodworking tools, such as hammers, nails, and pegs
- safety goggles

Gardening/nature

- cages with pets, such as rabbits, hamsters, and gerbils
- real gardening tools, rakes, gloves, and shovels
- watering cans
- bug box / bird feeder
- magnifying glass and binoculars
- loose parts (items children can move around, such as stones, twigs, slices of tree trunk, crates, and rope)

Other equipment/materials

- cubbies
- room dividers
- low, open shelving
- area rugs
- cots or sleeping mats
- cutlery for eating; serving bowls and pieces
- storage for adult items

Safety Reminders

All the equipment, materials, and toys in your program must meet these safety requirements:

- be free of sharp edges, splinters, lead paint, and other toxins
- pose no potential choking or suffocation hazards
- meet applicable safety guidelines issued by local, state, or tribal licensing agencies, Head Start, or military child development / Sure Start programs

Use the safety checklist in appendix A to ensure that the toys, materials, and equipment in your program are safe for preschoolers.

What Toys, Materials, and Equipment Should Look Like

In a high-quality preschool program, the materials and equipment in the indoor learning centers and outdoor space should be varied, developmentally appropriate, and inviting. They should enable children to work individually, with a peer, or in a small group to meet learning goals and standards.

In the following examples, you will see what quality measures should be in place when you observe the toys, materials, and equipment in a preschool program and why these measures are important.

What you should see	Why
Learning centers include toys and other items that respond to and build on children's interests.	One of the best ways to motivate learning is to build on children's interests. Children are eager to explore and experiment with playthings that allow them to focus on a special interest. This practice also gives children a message that they belong and their interests are valued in the learning community.
Every learning center includes toys, materials, and equipment that support a wide range of developmental levels. Children use some toys, materials, and equipment that are familiar and some that offer slightly greater challenges than each child's skill level.	Any group of preschoolers, ages three to five, is likely to include children at various levels of development. Learning centers should be stocked with materials that offer success (in playing with the familiar) and also challenge children and increase their skills without causing frustration.
There are sufficient toys and other materials available in each learning center to support the maximum number of children allowed to play there. For example, if the music and movement center is only large enough to support four children playing at one time, multiple materials are available, enabling all four children to choose what is of interest to them at their skill level.	Providing enough choices allows all of the children playing in a center to find something of interest to play with that is at their developmental level. At the same time, too many choices can be overwhelming and lead to frustration, especially for children who are stressed or unfamiliar with a group setting.
The toys, materials, and equipment displayed in each learning center represent only a part of the available inventory for that center.	Putting out the entire inventory would be overwhelming to children. To offer children manageable choices, it's best to display items that are of current interest and match their present and emerging skill levels.
Toys, materials, and equipment are rotated periodically as children get tired of them, develop new interests, and gain new skills.	Preschoolers are engaged in the ongoing process of gaining new skills, interests, and knowledge. Stocking the learning centers with fresh items builds on children's interests and experiences, and motivates them to explore and experiment with new ideas and content.

What you should see	Why
Toys and materials that are used together are displayed and stored together.	In a well-organized area, children can find what they need when they need it. For example, when collage materials are near papers, glue, and scissors, children can sit down and make a collage while their interest is high. They don't have to look for what they need.
Teachers add new toys, materials, and equipment to support the curriculum. For example, after a trip to a farm, they add rubber farm animals to the dramatic play center, farm animal lotto games to the math and manipulatives center, and books on farms to the literacy center.	Young children learn by revisiting and re-creating their experiences. Curriculum-related items allow children to reinforce and expand their learning, motivating them to learn more.
There are many open-ended play items, such as balls, blocks, and a doll house, that children can use in a variety of ways.	Open-ended materials can be used in different ways by different children. They inspire creativity and send children the message that there is more than one way to do things.
Homemade and natural items, such as pinecones, shells, and plants, that supplement the purchased inventory of toys, materials, and equipment.	A rich inventory of playthings does not have to be costly. Some of the best materials are those that are found in nature or are homemade, like maracas or milk carton blocks.
Children use "real" tools (for example, knives for cooking and hammers for woodworking) and safety gear under close supervision.	Children are eager to try on adult roles. Real tools and safety gear enable them to cook and do woodworking successfully, just like their family members do. In addition, when used with adult supervision, real tools are considered safer than play ones that might break or frustrate the child because they are ineffective.
Teachers and children bring indoor toys and materials, such as art supplies, books, and writing materials, outside regularly.	Children benefit from interacting with materials over time in different contexts. Bringing materials that are normally used indoors to the outdoor play area gives children a different perspective.
Books and writing materials are found in all learning centers—not just the literacy center.	Having related books and writing materials in all centers promotes children's language and literacy skills and communicates the purposes of print. For example, in the block area, children can reference books on buildings and draw blueprints. In the dramatic play center, children can thumb through magazines in a doctor's office waiting area, and the doctor can use paper and markers to write a prescription.

When you observe the twelve items noted above in place, it is likely that the equipment, toys, and materials in your program support the learning of preschoolers. Use the checklist in appendix D to observe how well your program meets these criteria. For items that your program is not yet addressing well, work with teachers to devise and implement an action plan for improvement. As a supervisor, you are responsible for ensuring that program toys, materials, and equipment optimally support children's growth, development, and learning.

When the Toys, Materials, and Equipment Need Further Adjusting

For deeper insight into the effectiveness of your program's equipment, toys, and materials, it's important to observe children using these items. It's one thing to have a well-thought-out, safe, and developmentally appropriate inventory, but unless these tools facilitate growth, development, and learning, the items are of little use. If you spot children engaged in behaviors such as those described below, the equipment, toys, and materials may be contributing to problems that hamper learning. Discuss with teachers the warning sign, reasons why the behavior might be happening, and the possible solutions noted in the third column. Help them implement these countermeasures or others they develop to make your program's toys, materials, and equipment more effective.

Note: Some of the warning signs listed below may be caused by factors other than the program's equipment, toys, and materials or by a combination of factors. Regular observations will provide information about the precise cause of the problem.

Warning sign	Why this might be happening	How educators can address the problem
Children angrily throw puzzle pieces.	The puzzles are too difficult and cause children to get frustrated when they can't succeed in putting them together.	Every child needs to succeed. Suggest that teachers review their observation notes and make sure the puzzles and other materials match the children's skill levels. In this case, offer puzzles with ten or fewer pieces to children who find doing puzzles challenging. As their skill levels increase, add puzzles with more pieces.
Children dress up in the dramatic play area, then go to other centers in search of accessories for their outfits.	Dress-up props are not grouped together, causing an interruption in children's play.	Schedule a time to work with teachers to take a critical look at all the centers. Survey the inventory, note how items are displayed, and ensure items used together are grouped together.
Children fight over popular toys, materials, and equipment.	There are not enough items to choose from. Or there are not duplicates of favorite toys and materials.	Together with teachers, survey all of the learning centers to make sure the inventory is sufficient. Also, to prevent conflicts, make sure that there are duplicates of the most popular toys and materials. Even though many preschoolers share well, some are still working on this skill.

Warning sign	Why this might be happening	How educators can address the problem
Children use items in a repetitive way, then lose interest quickly and move on to another activity or center, or sit doing nothing.	The items have not been rotated regularly. Or the playthings are too simple or too developmentally advanced.	Work with teachers to periodically replace items that are no longer of interest to children with new ones that tap into current interests and take cues from the curriculum. Also, make sure learning centers offer play materials that match each child's development.
Children gather in the same two or three centers every day.	The inventory in the other centers is not as appealing to children.	Lead teachers in taking a critical look at how children use the learning centers. Why are some centers popular and others unused? What can you do to attract children to all the centers? Is new inventory needed? Do the items need to be better organized and displayed?
Children depend on teachers for guidance on what toys, materials, or equipment to play with and how to play with them.	Items are not displayed so that children can use them independently. Or the toys, materials, or equipment are too difficult for children to play with on their own.	Help teachers arrange centers so items are well organized and labeled. Remind teachers to let children know they can get out, play with, and return items on their own. Ensure the inventory matches children's developmental levels.
Children ignore newly added equipment, such as a microscope in the science center.	Equipment has not been adequately introduced and children don't know how to use it and/or children are afraid of breaking it.	Underscore for teachers that while child choice is important, there is a place for direct teaching. When introducing a sophisticated piece of equipment such as a microscope, it's important that teachers model how to operate the device. They might start out by teaching a few children and ask those children to teach the others in the class until everyone is familiar with the equipment.
At the end of choice time, children place toys, materials, and equipment anywhere or dump items together on a shelf.	The toys, materials, and equipment are not displayed clearly with labels with both pictures and words, or items are not well grouped. Teachers may also be lax about children putting away their playthings when they are done using them.	Work with teachers to ensure that centers are appropriately organized and that play materials are well displayed. Encourage teachers to plan engaging ways—such as a cleanup song—to involve everyone in putting away things and getting ready for the next activity. Once they know what is expected, most preschoolers will take part in cleanup and take pride in their room.

Program Structure

The program structure provides the framework for the day's events. When followed consistently, this structure gives children a sense of security. The time allocated for each scheduled period should reflect a recognition of the needs, interests, and abilities of preschool children; for example, active and quiet periods should be balanced during the day. Because elaborate play where children explore concepts in depth requires large chunks of time, at least an hour of time needs to be offered for self-selected activities indoors and outdoors. Periods when preschool children are in a large group (such as morning or afternoon meetings) should be short—no more than twenty minutes. An appropriate program structure reflects the developmental abilities of the children.

Foundations Underlying Quality

Before observing your program's structure to ensure its effectiveness, you will need to be sure your program's schedule is appropriate for preschoolers and has an effective approach to carrying out transitions.

Sample Schedule for a Preschool Program

Many high-quality preschool programs are full day, typically for six hours or longer. This provides children with an opportunity to become involved in their play and reach expected learning goals. No one schedule fits all programs. Yours will depend on the amount of time allotted for the day and any fixed times, such as lunch. The schedule that follows, which can be tweaked to accommodate your needs, offers a suggested plan for organizing a full-day program that should meet the learning needs of all children (Colker 2009; Dodge et al. 2016).

Scheduled activity	Approximate length of time	What teachers do
Teacher planning time	30 minutes prior to opening	Review the day's plans, conduct health and safety checks, make sure all needed materials are out and available to children. Wash hands.
Arrival	10 minutes	Greet individual children and family members. Exchange information with family members. Have children use attendance chart, store belongings, wash hands, and select an activity.
Morning group meeting	20 minutes	Talk about what children did the previous evening/weekend. Assign children jobs for the day. Go over daily schedule. Read story, sing song or do fingerplay.

Scheduled activity	Approximate length of time	What teachers do
Indoor choice time	60 minutes	Move through centers, interacting with individual children in ways that extend learning. Lead small-group activities (sometimes family member volunteers do this too). Remind children to clean up after they are through using an item and make sure that every child who wants a snack has one. Help children put on jackets, if needed, to go outdoors.
Outdoor choice time	60 minutes	Carefully supervise gross-motor play. Interact with children in individual and small-group activities, such as reading a book, drawing with sidewalk chalk, or tending a garden.
Storytime and lunch preparation	15 minutes	Oversee children hanging up jackets, using the toilet, and washing hands. One teacher reads a story to the group while another teacher works with helpers to set tables for family-style lunch.
Lunch	45 minutes	Sit at tables with children, conversing about the day's events, nutrition, and other topics raised by the children. Guide children in cleaning up, washing hands, brushing teeth, and getting ready for rest time. Teachers help children place mats/cots where desired.
Rest time	60 minutes	Help children relax and fall asleep. Teachers give children a book or quiet playthings if they cannot sleep and choose to rest.
Indoor or outdoor choice time	45 minutes	Help children put away their mats/cots and blankets as they wake up, use the toilet and wash their hands, serve themselves a snack, and choose a quiet activity indoors or play outdoors with a supervising teacher. Teachers interact with individual children as they snack and play.
Afternoon group meeting/departure	15 minutes	Lead circle time, reviewing the day's activities and any new concepts children may have learned. Assist children as they clean up, locate work to take home, and get outdoor clothing. Help children transition to their families as needed, and exchange information with family members. Say good-bye to all, highlighting something special about each child. Reassure children whose parents have not arrived yet.
Debriefing	30 minutes or as time allows	Review the day, work on children's portfolios, and plan for the next day.

Transitions

Transitions are the in-between times when children move from one activity to the next—from indoor to outdoor activities, from outdoor play to lunch preparation and lunchtime, from lunchtime to rest time, and the like. Transitions can become problem periods if children don't know what is expected of them. Waiting is difficult for young children, and unless they are engaged in something interesting, they might find something to do that does not fit in with the teachers' plans.

To make transitions easier, teachers can plan for them. Here are some ideas on how to do this:

☀ **Make sure children know ahead of time when transitions are coming.** Point out where on the schedule transitions occur. "Before we have lunch, we'll hang up our jackets, use the toilet and wash our hands, and sit down in the block center where I'll read you a story."

☀ **Provide notice.** Give children a five-minute warning that they need to put their playthings away, get their jackets, and line up to go outside. In some programs this is one of the daily jobs for children. The "reminder" person goes to each learning center to announce the coming transition.

☀ **Use visual cues.** Hold up a backpack to alert children that it's time to go home.

☀ **Give clear and age-appropriate directions.** "Please scrape food from your plate into the trash can and then go to the bathroom to wash your hands and brush your teeth."

☀ **Use transitions as learning opportunities.** "If your name starts with the same beginning sound as Mother, Milk, and Monkey, please go get your jacket and stand in line."

☀ **Give children specific tasks.** "Will today's lunch helpers please get the plates and glasses off the lunch cart and bring them to the table in the art center?"

☀ **Be flexible.** If children are engrossed in building a space station out of blocks, let them work on the project a while longer or find a way to leave the structure up and protected so they can return to it later.

What Program Structure Should Look Like

In a high-quality preschool program, the program structure supports and enhances children's growth, development, and learning. The daily schedule allows children to become deeply involved in activities and projects and to transition from quiet to active play. Routines and transitions are integrated into learning activities. Everything that happens during the day supports children's mastery of learning standards.

In the chart below, you will find examples of an appropriate program structure and how it supports the progress of preschool children.

What you should see	Why
Time slots for daily activities match children's developmental capabilities.	Ensuring that scheduled time slots match children's developmental abilities reduces the likelihood of behavior problems. For example, most preschoolers cannot sit with a group for longer than twenty minutes. A longer time slot would likely lead to children being bored, losing focus, or fidgeting.
Active and quiet times are alternated throughout the day. For example, indoor child choice time is followed by physically active time outdoors.	Young children learn through both quiet and physically active play. An appropriate schedule alternates these times to give children an opportunity to recoup the energy expended during gross-motor play by doing quiet activities. Once refreshed, children feel renewed and are eager to engage in active play again.
Children play outdoors at least once a day for at least an hour.	Being outdoors every day for extended periods of time is crucial to children's health and learning. An hour-long outdoor time allows children to make and carry out their plans.
Children spend at least an hour engaged in activities of their own choosing, including working on projects and interacting with teachers.	Children learn best when they can select activities that are of interest to them and when they have time to make plans and investigate, explore, experiment, and pretend. Children can develop increasingly complex thinking skills when they have time to fully interact with materials and people.
Cleanup is ongoing rather than being a separate item on the daily schedule.	Children can learn to return toys and materials as they use them and will enjoy feeling responsible for keeping the room tidy. When cleanup is an ongoing activity, less time is needed to prepare for the next transition.
Children eat morning and afternoon snacks when they are hungry; snacks are part of child choice time rather than being a separate item on the daily schedule.	Part of learning about nutrition during the preschool years is recognizing feelings of thirst and hunger. Self-served snacks promote independence and involve children in food preparation. At the same time, they can develop social, math, language, and fine-motor skills. By having children who have snacked "sign" their names on a sheet of paper, teachers can monitor who has had a snack and encourage those who haven't eaten to do so.
Children transition in small groups from being outdoors to getting ready to eat lunch. For example, one group hangs up their coats while another group uses the toilet and washes their hands.	Transitioning in small groups helps children de-stress and relax in preparation for a comforting lunch. Children can take their time using the bathroom and washing their hands because they are not rushed.

What you should see	Why
At mealtimes, adults and children pass bowls of food around the table and serve themselves family-style.	When children are allowed to serve themselves, they learn to judge what and how much they want to eat, at the same time developing fine-motor skills.
Teachers and visiting family members eat a relaxed, nutritious meal with small groups of children, engaging them in conversation. Adults encourage—but do not force—children to try all offered foods.	Children enjoy and digest their food better when things are calm and inviting. Through conversation, they acquire social skills, learn about nutrition, and develop thinking skills. In a relaxed atmosphere, they are more likely to be willing to try new, healthy foods.
Children seamlessly transition from lunch to rest time as they finish eating.	Not all children eat at the same pace. Rather than imposing a strict time frame on eating, allowing each child to determine how long she will take to eat is healthier. Preschoolers can clear their dirty dishes and trays, use the bathroom, wash hands, brush their teeth, and place their mats in a preferred space, with a teacher's help if needed.
Children nap according to their own time clocks for as long as needed. As children wake up, they roll up their mats or put away their cots, help themselves to a snack, and choose a quiet activity for play.	A one-hour rest time is sufficient for most preschoolers. Some children may not sleep at all and will use this time to rest, while others regularly need a longer nap, particularly if they do not feel well or have not slept well the night before. A child's well-being takes precedence over the schedule.
Teachers give sufficient warning to children when a transition is about to take place. For example, "In five minutes it will be time for our afternoon group meeting. Now is the time to finish up what you are working on."	Preschool children can become very involved in activities and find it difficult to stop and change directions. Transitions work smoother when children are prepared. Children are more likely to cooperate when they are given a warning and have time to complete what they have started.

When you observe the twelve items noted above in place, it is likely that your program's schedule is serving preschoolers well. Use the checklist in appendix D to observe how well your program meets these criteria. For items that your program is not yet addressing well, work with teachers to devise and implement an action plan for improvement. As a supervisor, you are responsible for ensuring that the program structure optimally supports children's growth, development, and learning.

When the Program Structure Needs Further Adjusting

For deeper insight into the effectiveness of your program's structure, it's important to observe children and teachers throughout the entire day. It's one thing to have a well-thought-out schedule on paper, but unless the schedule allows children the time they need to be involved in activities and transition smoothly from one activity to the next, it is of little use. If you spot children and teachers engaged in behaviors such as those described below, the program schedule may need adjusting. Discuss with teachers the warning sign, reasons why the behavior might be happening, and the possible solutions noted in the third column. Help them implement these countermeasures or others they develop to make your program's schedule more effective.

Note: Some of the warning signs listed below may be caused by factors other than the program's structure or by a combination of the program structure and other factors. Regular observations will provide information about the precise cause of the problem.

Warning sign	Why this might be happening	How educators can address the problem
Children seem confused about what comes next during the day and resist transitioning to the next activity.	There is only a written schedule posted that children cannot read. Or teachers do not prepare children for an upcoming change of activity.	Encourage teachers to take photos of the children during daily routines and activities, and use them to make picture schedules posted at the children's eye level. Work with the teachers to plan how to introduce and regularly refer to the schedule so children know what comes next each day. They can use the photo schedule to help children develop a sense of time and sequencing. In addition, help teachers plan special songs or transition activities. They can use the picture schedule as an aid.
Teachers make attendance-taking a group activity, which eats into morning meeting time.	Teachers feel pressured to provide accurate and timely attendance reports to the administrative office. Or teachers think that children learn from the activity.	Suggest attendance strategies that will not intrude on morning meeting time. For example, teachers can make a wall chart with two columns: one labeled "Home" and the other labeled "School." Under each column glue Velcro strips. Then make a card with each child's photo on the front and Velcro on the back. Upon arrival, children can move their photo from the Home column to the School column. Use English and home languages on the chart as appropriate.
Children look around, fidget, or get up and walk away from the group meeting while the teacher presents a lengthy introduction to a song or fingerplay.	Teachers are not aware that developmentally, most preschoolers cannot sit focused in a group for more than twenty minutes. When the meeting is too long, they lose focus and need to move their bodies.	Review the schedule with teachers and discuss why group meetings are allotted a twenty-minute time span. Brainstorm some activities that can be introduced to small groups of children, rather than the whole group at once. Model this kind of teaching when visiting the room.

Warning sign	Why this might be happening	How educators can address the problem
Teachers cancel outdoor time on cold days or hot days. By the end of the morning, children are running around the room and having physical disagreements.	Children have pent-up energy from being indoors all morning. Teachers do not recognize the importance of going outdoors every day, regardless of the temperature (unless the weather poses a health danger). Perhaps children did not bring clothing that is appropriate for the weather.	Stress the importance of having outdoor time daily. In winter make sure there are extra mittens, hats, and scarves for children. If the weather truly becomes too cold or hot to go outdoors, seek out indoor alternatives for gross-motor activity, such as a gym or activity room if there is not a designated gross-motor area in the classroom.
Teachers scold children for getting out of line while waiting for their peers to put on their jackets to go outdoors.	Teachers do not handle transitions well. They try to maintain order by having the whole group get ready to go outside at the same time.	Offer print and digital resources with ideas for ensuring smooth transitions. Ask teachers to try out and report back on effective strategies, such as asking everyone who is wearing the color red today to get in line. Congratulate teachers when they make transitions both an opportunity to learn and a fun activity.
Teachers use choice time as an opportunity to finish their own paperwork or get materials ready for a future activity.	Teachers believe that during choice time, children can and should do everything on their own. Teachers do not recognize the vital role they play with children during choice time by interacting with them and extending their learning.	With the teachers' permission, video record teachers and children at play during choice time. Watch the video with individual teachers to identify times they extended children's learning and when opportunities were missed. Discuss how to be aware of those opportunities in the future. Later on, video record the teachers again to validate their successes.
Teachers put food on children's plates at mealtime and snacktime and tell children to eat everything on their plates.	Teachers do not understand the purpose of family-style dining and making snack a part of choice time—to help children be independent and responsible for their own nutrition. Additionally, teachers may find it more efficient to take control themselves.	Hold a workshop to model family-style dining by eating together, as teachers do with the children. When teachers are ready, observe each one joining a group of four to six children for a family-style meal. After the observation, share your notes, and together identify what went well and what could be improved. Hold a similar workshop on including the morning and afternoon snack as a choice activity in the cooking center. Children prepare and help themselves to the suggested snack (such as two celery sticks, four orange wedges, and a glass of milk). After eating, children clean up after themselves and "sign" a sheet showing they have eaten.
Children who have finished eating remain at the table, waiting for their peers to finish eating.	Teachers think it's polite for children to wait for classmates who eat more slowly, and that by enforcing this rule, they are helping children learn manners.	Reassure teachers that learning this polite behavior can come when children are older. Right now they are just not developmentally ready to sit and wait, especially when they are tired and ready for naps.

Curriculum: Activities and Experiences

An early childhood curriculum is a written framework that guides teaching and learning. It acts as a blueprint for what you want your program to be. Like the title of this book, it provides the what, why, and how of implementing a high-quality learning program for children. Preschool curricula focus on children's mastery of skills in all learning domains through play in indoor and outdoor learning centers. When you use the curriculum, the activities and experiences you offer children are never random but are part of a well-thought-out plan for achieving your program's goals and objectives, as well as addressing early learning standards.

Foundations Underlying Quality

Before observing teachers implementing the curriculum with preschoolers, you will need to be sure your program has a high-quality curriculum in place. Because preschool programs have differing goals and missions, there is no one curriculum that every preschool program should use. Some programs design their own curriculum to meet specific needs and circumstances. Others select and purchase a curriculum such as Teaching Strategies' *The Creative Curriculum for Preschool*, *The HighScope Preschool Curriculum*, or *Tools of the Mind* (Third Sector New England), which are research-based and validated.

A high-quality preschool curriculum guides teachers, administrators, and families as they work together to support and maximize children's development and learning. Whether program-designed or a standardized commercial one, your curriculum should meet these criteria:

* It is consistent with your program's goals and objectives.

* It is aligned with mandated standards, be they federal (in the case of Head Start and military child development programs / Sure Start) state, local, or tribal agency.

* There is documented evidence of the curriculum's success in helping children achieve early learning standards.

* It promotes development in all learning domains: social, emotional, physical, language, and cognitive.

* There is an organized scope and sequence for each of the learning domains noted above. Scope and sequence refer to the ideas, concepts, and topics that will be covered in the curriculum.

* It details how to set up the environment to facilitate independence, initiative, and choice.

* The roles and expectations for teachers are described in depth.

* Children have many opportunities to explore the world and experiment through play.

* The learning activities include both child-guided and adult-guided strategies.

* Learning activities allow children to play alone, in pairs, in small groups, and in full groups.

* Teaching strategies are differentiated, based on individual skills, abilities, temperaments, interests, learning preferences, home languages, family structure, and culture.

* It can be tailored to support children with specific disabilities.

* Teachers and families are considered partners in their children's learning at the program and at home.

* Observationally based assessment is used to document and measure children's progress.

What the Curriculum Should Look Like

In a high-quality program, the curriculum is implemented as it was designed to be used. Teachers may make adaptations to fit the makeup of their program, but they adhere to the curriculum's stated goals, objectives, and mission. In the chart below, you will find examples of what the routines, experiences, and activities in a high-quality preschool curriculum would look like and why.

What you should see	Why
Children work independently on tasks or activities that they have selected for themselves, such as putting together a puzzle in the math and manipulatives center, weaving ribbons through a fence outdoors, or looking at a book while seated on a beanbag chair in a loft. Teachers interact with children by asking open-ended questions and making comments and suggestions as appropriate.	When children are allowed to select an activity in a center of their choice, they are naturally encouraged to learn. By observing what children are doing, teachers can extend children's learning by questioning and offering suggestions. For example, "I see that you have created a pattern with the bottle tops—large, small, small, large. What other patterns could you create?"
Children work in pairs or small groups on cooperative activities of their choosing, such as making an airport out of blocks, re-creating a trip to a farm in the dramatic play area, or looking for worms under a rock outdoors. Teachers pose questions and make suggestions as needed.	By working on activities with their peers, children naturally learn social skills. In addition, as Lev Vygotsky theorized, children learn new skills from peers who are more advanced than they are. For example, children who cooperatively build a skyscraper out of blocks will likely make a sturdier, more elaborate creation than either child could do alone.

What you should see	Why
Children are engaged in project-related work (such as a study of ants) either individually, in pairs, or in small groups. Teachers pose questions that inspire children's investigations and document children's work with photos and written notes.	Project work is a way of organizing content to make it both relevant and exciting. It is an especially useful curricular tool for preschoolers because it responds to their interests, allows for self-direction, and supports learning in all domains, including the social-emotional. Children can study ants, for example, by looking at them outdoors using magnifying glasses. An individual child in the science center might track an ant's route in an ant farm and then make a chart of its movements. In the literacy center, a teacher might read a library book on ant colonies to the group. In the music and movement center, children could move like ants to a recording of "The Ants Go Marching." Throughout the study, teachers observe and record children's questions and comments, photograph their creations, and collect work samples to document progress.
Teachers regularly observe children's interactions and activities, document what they see and hear, and maintain individual portfolios. Using these observations, teachers steer children to activities that are a good fit for their development and interests.	Observation is a key way to collect the information needed to plan an individualized preschool curriculum that offers opportunities to practice skills a child has mastered and gain new skills. Observations also are used for accountability purposes and to demonstrate success in addressing early learning standards.
Children play with peers, exhibiting behaviors such as sharing, friendship, and empathy. Teachers model these behaviors and support children's positive behaviors.	Socio-emotional skills are vital to children's well-being and their success in school. When children play with peers and participate as members of a learning community, they learn to respect differences and control their emotions (self-regulation).
Children use their large muscles in various activities throughout the day, such as climbing up a slide outdoors, marching with musical instruments in the music and movement center, and leaping like a frog as part of a transition activity.	Gross-motor development is a major focus of learning for preschoolers. Teachers should engage children in activities both indoors and outdoors that will help them master and develop new movement skills like throwing and kicking balls, skipping, leaping, hopping, and riding bikes.
Children use the small muscles in their hands in various activities throughout the day, such as guiding a computer mouse, writing their names, building with Lego blocks, or hulling strawberries for a cooking activity.	Fine-motor development is another major focus of learning for preschoolers. When every learning center includes materials that require use of small muscles, children can master skills, strengthen their hand and finger muscles, improve eye-hand coordination, and prepare for writing.

What you should see	Why
Children take part in conversations and view print and its uses in English and in their home language throughout the day. They do this, for example, by participating in a dramatic play scenario as a doctor questioning a patient, making a sign to keep their block creation undisturbed in the block center, and dictating to a teacher what their painting is about in the art center.	The development of language and literacy skills is an important goal for preschoolers. Having a print-rich environment with books in every learning center allows children to expand their language skills and gain a foundation for reading and writing. Having print in both English and children's home languages enables children to retain and gain new skills in both languages.
Children solve problems (how to make a wire sculpture that stands up without falling over), explore cause and effect (what happens when you hurt a friend), and apply old knowledge to new situations (trying out new objects during a sink and float activity) throughout the day.	Preschoolers can build their thinking skills during routines, transitions, activities, and in learning centers at choice time. Teachers facilitate cognitive development by providing open-ended materials and interacting with children by narrating the child's actions and results, asking questions, and making suggestions. They also plan activities with specific cognitive goals in mind.
Children express their ideas and feelings through the creative arts. For example, children make up a puppet show based on a story their teacher read to them, re-create the dance they saw during a field trip to a community college performance, and try out different painting techniques using tools other than brushes.	A high-quality preschool curriculum strikes a balance between academic subjects (literacy, math, science, and social studies), developing social and emotional skills, the arts (dramatic art, visual art, music, and dance), and building physical skills and fitness. Moreover, as the Reggio Emilia–inspired programs have so well demonstrated, the arts provide a springboard for learning. Recognizing and repeating musical patterns, for example, facilitates children's understanding of mathematical patterns.
Teachers ensure that the curriculum is accessible to all children, including those with special needs. For example, they allow a child who cannot concentrate to leave the morning meeting and work with another teacher, add books on raccoons to the literacy center to respond to a child who is fascinated by the animal, and adapt painting and drawing tools so a child with orthopedic impairments can fully participate in art projects.	Every child has unique strengths and challenges, interests, and motivators. A high-quality curriculum encourages teachers to individualize materials, the environment, interactions, and whatever else will ensure the child has full access to the program. This does not mean that each child needs his own curriculum. Rather, it means that teachers adapt the same curriculum so it is accessible to each child.
Family members share their skills and interests and play with, read to, and otherwise engage the children. For example, a parent leads a small group in a game of lotto, a grandmother helps the children plant a garden, or a parent joins the class on a nature walk.	Research shows that when families partner with early childhood programs, children learn more and feel more competent and confident. It is important that family members feel welcomed by the program and are encouraged to volunteer during the day when children can see them working together with their teachers.

When you observe the twelve items noted above in place, it is likely that your program's curriculum is serving preschoolers well. Use the checklist in appendix D to observe how well your program meets these criteria. For items that your program is not yet addressing well, work with teachers to devise and implement an action plan for improvement. As a supervisor, you are responsible for ensuring that the curriculum optimally supports children's growth, development, and learning.

When the Curriculum Needs Further Adjusting

For deeper insight into the effectiveness of your program's curriculum, it's important to observe children and teachers at various times throughout the day. To be fully effective, a high-quality curriculum should be implemented as it was designed to be used, with fidelity. If, for example, your program believes that in using the chosen preschool curriculum you should not include children with disabilities because it would be "too difficult" for them to participate, this would be a misuse of the curriculum—as well as a discriminatory practice.

If you spot children and teachers engaged in behaviors such as those described below, the curriculum's implementation may need adjusting. Discuss with teachers the warning sign, reasons why the behavior might be happening, and the possible solutions noted in the third column. Help them implement these countermeasures or others they develop to make your program's implementation of the curriculum more effective.

Note: Some of the warning signs listed below may be caused by factors other than implementation problems or a combination of curriculum implementation problems and other factors. Regular observations will provide information about the precise cause of the problem.

Warning sign	Why this might be happening	How educators can address the problem
Teachers assign children to specific learning centers.	Teachers are trying to match children's interests and skills to what the centers offer. Or teachers are encouraging children to try centers they haven't wanted to use. Or teachers mistakenly think this is appropriate practice.	Discuss with teachers the importance of having children choose the center they want to play in (it is one effective way to ensure children are motivated to learn). If a child tends to play only in one center, brainstorm with teachers other ways to solve this issue. For example, they could put materials of interest to a child in several centers and then invite the child to play with those materials in a new center.
Teachers have children move to a new center every ten minutes.	Teachers don't understand that children need sufficient time to both plan and carry out their plans during choice time. They may mistakenly think children should play in as many centers as possible each day.	Hold a workshop to review the purpose and use of learning centers. Ask the group to consider how long they think it takes a child to become fully engaged in building a block tower or acting out a dramatic play scenario. Discuss the need to let children have extended play in a center to master higher-level skills. Also, make the point that it's not necessary for a child to play in more than a single learning center each day. It's the level of play that is important, not the number of centers in which the child plays.
Teachers rush through routines such as putting on / taking off coats, eating meals, and brushing teeth.	Teachers believe that all learning occurs during activities in learning centers and that routines are "downtime."	With the teachers' permission, video record teachers during routines. Then, watch the videos individually with each teacher and discuss how she or he might have taken better advantage of these times to make them learning opportunities for children. At a later time, make follow-up videos to highlight teachers successfully using routines as teaching opportunities.
Children resist and refuse to use the designated green crayon during a project to color a Christmas tree stencil.	Teachers have a vision of what the holiday bulletin board should look like. They have planned an activity that will have the children make the standard items they need for the vision.	Even teachers who know better sometimes get carried away—especially at holiday time. Brainstorm with teachers ways to involve families in deciding which holidays to celebrate and how to celebrate them. For example, celebrations might include making art, tasting special foods, and other activities. There are two issues to address. First, holidays should be sensitive to all children's heritages, and not everyone celebrates Christmas. Second, stencils, teacher-made projects, and "correct" color crayons are not developmentally appropriate because they do not encourage children to use their own creativity.

Warning sign	Why this might be happening	How educators can address the problem
Children play within stereotypical gender roles—boys play with trucks and trains and girls play with dolls.	Teachers may believe that boys and girls prefer different toys and perhaps subconsciously have steered children to play with toys that they feel are gender appropriate. Teachers and families may come from cultures in which children of all ages are expected to stay within accepted gender roles.	Meet with teachers and have them share their thoughts about gender roles and toys and what they think families believe about this issue. Discuss what messages children learn by trying out different roles, both through toys and in dramatic play. Ask them to reflect on how they might inadvertently send messages about appropriate gender-related behaviors. If it is culturally appropriate, challenge teachers to consciously promote use of all toys and roles by both boys and girls.
Teachers speak only English to children.	Teachers are fluent only in English and don't feel competent speaking other languages. They may feel that having print in children's home languages is enough to make all children comfortable. Or teachers think that immersing children in English is the best approach.	Underscore how important it is for preschoolers who are learning two languages to hear the important people in their lives speaking both their home language and English. Encourage teachers to learn a few key words in all of the children's home languages. If teachers have trouble with the pronunciation, try writing sentence strips in the children's home languages—with a phonetic version underneath—of questions or comments they might ask children. Visitors to the program will find these helpful too.
Children get frustrated and upset when they are unable to sign and spell their names correctly on their drawings.	Teachers know that having children sign their names is often an early learning standard for preschool. They are trying to get all of the children in the class to do this, even when some are not yet developmentally ready to do so.	Provide ongoing training for teachers on the use of early learning standards. Underscore that these are goals—not requirements—and what is most important is that preschoolers make progress. Not every preschooler will master every goal, but every child should be making progress toward the goals. Discuss how to help children gain the skills they need to ultimately be able to achieve a given goal. Stress that a teacher's job is to meet each child at his developmental level and work with him to increase his skills. Children need to be encouraged, not frustrated, and teachers need to have appropriate expectations.
Children fidget and leave the circle at meeting time.	Teachers expect all children to be able to stay in the circle for the whole meeting. Or the meeting time lasts longer than twenty minutes. Or the group meeting is not well run or of interest to the children.	Review the purpose and procedures for running effective circle time meetings. Most preschoolers can attend for only twenty minutes or so. If a child does not feel like participating, offer an alternative activity. Brainstorm appropriate activities that will keep children engaged in the meeting.

Supportive Interactions

The atmosphere in a high-quality preschool program reflects the tone and content of the interactions. Lively chatter can be heard as children talk and work together and teachers respond to their ideas, questions, and concerns. Teachers display genuine interest in what the children are doing, how they are feeling, and what they have to say. The teachers' expectations for individual children are appropriate to what those children can understand and do at their stages of development and to individual characteristics, such as culture, family structure, and home language. An atmosphere of cooperation and caring prevails.

Foundations Underlying Quality

What kinds of supportive interactions might a visitor to a preschool room look for? What are the signs that teachers' words and actions foster preschoolers' growth, development, and learning? How will the visitor know that the preschoolers are exploring, learning, and guiding much of their own learning in this setting? Teachers' supportive interactions with preschoolers share the following characteristics.

- ☼ Teachers listen carefully to preschoolers' ideas, comments, requests, and questions. If appropriate, a teacher might rephrase what the preschooler said to ensure she or he heard it clearly. Only after the child has finished talking does the teacher respond with a comment or question that keeps a conversation going or leads to a higher level of thinking and learning. For example, "You asked, 'How many different kinds of birds have been tasting the suet feeders we made and hung last week?' What could you do to find the answer to that question?"

- ☼ Teachers offer suggestions without taking over the child's activity. They respond to the child's interests first, introducing new ideas if they fit with the child's plans. Their suggestions often plant a seed, encouraging the child to come up with her own creative ideas. For example, a teacher might ask, "Could you use a paper towel roll to make a telescope?" to which the child responds, "Yeah, but the wrapping paper rolls are longer. I'm going to use one of those."

- ☼ Teachers notice and comment on preschoolers' progress in learning something new, gaining a skill, or completing a project. They invite children to describe their goals and the steps they are taking to achieve them. For example, the teacher might say, "Sara, I saw you walking on the balance beam today. You got halfway across. How did you stay balanced?" Then Sara may respond, "I put my arms out to the side and looked straight ahead."

- ☼ Teachers provide scaffolding—just enough of the right kind of support to help children develop skills and learn content. For example, "If you hold the hammer closer to the end, you may find it easier to hit the nail."

But most of all, supportive interactions tell preschoolers, "I see you playing and learning with your friends. You are competent, interesting, kind, and capable of doing many things by yourself and with a little help. You are a valuable member of our class, your family, and your community."

What Supportive Interactions Should Look Like

In a high-quality preschool room, teachers invite children to share their ideas and questions. They let children know that they are good thinkers who know a lot and can apply their knowledge to learn new things. They encourage children to talk with and learn from each other. Look for the following strategies and outcomes when visiting a preschool room.

What you should see	Why
Teachers engage with children one-on-one, in a small groups, and as the entire class.	Teachers should spend most of the day talking with and fostering the learning of preschoolers through a variety of groupings, depending on the content and focus of their interactions. One-on-one interactions can be tailored to an individual child's interests and abilities, small groups work well for planned activities or when engaging with children at play during choice time, and full class interactions work well when teachers want to share information with or invite participation of all of the children in the group.
Teachers respond quickly and positively to children's needs and questions, comfort distressed children, and help them deal with their problems constructively.	Preschoolers develop a sense of trust and self-esteem when adults are responsive to their needs. They learn that they are important and worthy people.
Teachers bend, kneel, or sit down to establish eye contact when talking with children.	When culturally appropriate, eye contact promotes good communication. Preschoolers feel more respected when adults are at their level.
Teachers attend to children who are less verbal as well as to those who have a lot to say and who seek their attention.	Children who are quiet are sometimes overlooked, but they also need the attention of adults. When teachers make a point to get to know each child, they are more likely to address each child's needs.
Teachers show respect for children's feelings and ideas, even if they disagree with them.	When teachers acknowledge and show respect for children's feelings, children learn that they are valued, which enhances their self-esteem.
Teachers plan activities that encourage children to cooperate, work together, help each other, and care for one another.	Social competence is an underlying goal of early childhood education. Children who learn to work with others and develop friendships are more likely to succeed in school and in life.

What you should see	Why
Teachers model and encourage children to listen to other points of view and accept individual differences.	The ability to see things from another perspective is an important cognitive skill and is critical to living successfully in a group.
Teachers encourage and offer suggestions so children can solve problems on their own, make progress, complete challenging tasks, and learn from their mistakes.	Encouragement and support promote children's confidence, self-esteem, and understanding of new concepts. Children who feel good about themselves are more likely to attempt challenges that will help them develop new skills.
Teachers help children make friends and support their efforts to renegotiate friendships as necessary.	The ability to make friends and renegotiate friendships is central to children's overall health and well-being. Children who leave the preschool years feeling friendless are likely to experience social and learning problems in later life.
Teachers and children play, smile, laugh, and have fun while learning together.	A preschool classroom is most effective when the children and adults enjoy being a part of a joyful learning community.
Teachers support each other by keeping in touch during the day through gestures, facial expressions, and words.	A collegial atmosphere is critical to providing a safe place for learning. Children watch and learn from adults, and will notice and copy their use of social skills, such as cooperation, problem solving, and empathy.
Teachers and families give each other warm greetings and updates about the child's experiences and progress at home and at school.	Children thrive when they see the important adults in their lives—teachers and families—respecting each other and sharing information about them.

When you observe the twelve items noted above in place, it is likely that the interactions in your program are supportive and are fostering the development and learning of preschoolers. Use the checklist in appendix D to observe how well your program meets these criteria. For items that your program is not yet addressing well, work with teachers to devise and implement an action plan for improvement. As a supervisor, you are responsible for ensuring that teachers' supportive interactions foster children's growth, development, and learning.

When Interactions Need Further Adjusting

For deeper insight into the effectiveness of the supportive interactions between teachers and preschoolers, it's important to observe in the classroom. If you spot warning signs such as those in the examples described below, it's time to look more closely and try to identify what might be causing the situation. Discuss the possible solutions noted in the third column with teachers and help them better understand how supportive interactions nurture and foster the growth, development, and learning of preschoolers.

Note: Some of the warning signs listed below may be caused by factors other than nonsupportive interactions or by a combination of nonsupportive interactions and other factors. Regular observations will provide information about the precise cause of the problem.

Warning sign	Why this might be happening	How educators can address the problem
Teachers' interactions with children frequently focus on giving instructions or correcting mistakes.	Teachers may not realize that they seldom encourage or congratulate children for their efforts. They may not know the importance of interactions—to support learning and to build language skills.	Visit the classroom, and with the teacher's permission, video record for thirty minutes during choice time. Watch the video individually with each teacher and discuss his or her interactions with children. Focus on what goes well, while nudging the teacher to be more supportive. Point out specific examples of when support could have been more effective. At a later time, again video record choice time to identify successful teacher-child interactions.
Teachers require children to work and play quietly, and get upset when play is noisy.	Teachers might believe they are preparing children for elementary school, where they will be expected to work quietly. Or they may not realize that playful learning is not quiet—children must talk to each other, share ideas, make plans, ask and answer questions, and so on.	Reinforce the importance of play as a vehicle for learning in the preschool years, and discuss the characteristics of playful learning—including that it is often messy and noisy. Review the ways in which preschool does prepare children for further learning, by teaching them to solve problems, share ideas, cooperate, and make and carry out plans together.

Warning sign	Why this might be happening	How educators can address the problem
Teachers ignore some children and favor others by spending time with them.	Teachers probably do "like" some children better than others. They may not realize that their preferences are showing.	Observe teachers in the classroom. Share your observations with individual teachers, providing concrete examples of times they responded to one child but not another or answered one child's question while ignoring another child's request. Discuss professionalism and the importance of getting to know and support the learning of all of the children in the group. Offer to help if a teacher has trouble interacting with a child who is just not easy to like.
Teachers use only one teaching strategy—direct instruction—regardless of the content being addressed.	Teachers may worry that the children will not be able to achieve early learning standards unless they tell them what they need to know. They may fear for their own job security or worry that the children won't do well in kindergarten.	Share examples of what kindergarten teachers hope children will be able to do when they enter school. Typically, when asked, kindergarten teachers mention social and emotional skills rather than content. Reassure the preschool teachers that they do not have to "pour" information into preschoolers. Young children are eager learners whose play, explorations, experiences, conversations, and interactions lead to much content learning. Also, learning standards can't be taught. Children need to internalize knowledge and relate it to what they already know.
Teachers praise children, using generic phrases such as "good job."	Teachers may have experienced similar forms of praise when they were growing up. They may just be repeating what they heard from their own teachers and families, not realizing that phrases such as "good job" are empty words to young children.	Encourage and help teachers break the "good job" habit and learn to use evaluative praise that describes what the child did or achieved. Have teachers practice what they can say instead of "good job." Share and discuss this article about alternatives to saying "good job": www.naeyc.org/tyc/article/good-job-alternatives

Warning sign	Why this might be happening	How educators can address the problem
Teachers mispronounce the names of children and families whose home language is new to them or difficult to pronounce.	Working with families from diverse cultures may be a new experience for teachers. Perhaps they do not realize that learning to correctly pronounce names is an important way of showing respect for the family and the child.	Have teachers learn how to pronounce the first and last names of every child in their care. They can learn from the family or by searching online to find out how a name is pronounced. Provide index cards and markers so they can write phonetic versions of the names and encourage them to practice until they can welcome each child and family with a correctly pronounced greeting.
Teachers expect and try to teach children skills they are not yet ready to learn.	Teachers may lack sufficient knowledge of child development to understand that every child follows a unique timetable for development. They expect all three-year-olds, for example, to be able to pedal a tricycle. They may not be aware of the order in which skills typically develop.	Offer a variety of print and digital resources on child development, milestones, and scope and sequence. Reassure teachers that if they provide appropriate materials and encouragement and sufficient time, children will progress at their own pace of development and learning.
Teachers have poor relationships with colleagues; they are uncooperative and unpleasant to each other and use a harsh tone of voice when speaking with each other.	Teachers may have unresolved disagreements with, false assumptions about, or poor attitudes toward colleagues. They may not have time in the schedule for joint planning or sharing information about the children.	Plan teachers meetings that are focused on helping teachers get to know each other, their interests—possibly shared—and their goals for children. Note that children are keen observers who notice and learn from the classroom atmosphere. When the emotional environment is tense and unpleasant, children often feel anxious and are unable to fully engage in the program. Children learn positive communication by witnessing their teachers communicating in friendly ways. Make sure the program's orientation and planning processes are effective; make changes if they are not.

Positive Guidance

In a high-quality preschool program, the teachers support development and learning, including learning what behaviors are acceptable. They help children develop social and emotional skills and apply them to express feelings, make requests, and play and learn with their peers. The teachers have appropriate expectations for preschoolers and set limits that keep the children safe while allowing them to take full advantage of a well-stocked inventory of learning materials and opportunities to explore interests in depth. Through positive guidance, teachers help preschoolers assume greater responsibility for their own behavior and develop self-regulation skills to use now and in the future.

Self-regulation—the ability to control bodily functions, manage powerful emotions, maintain focus and attention, and delay gratification—is an important goal during the early childhood years. Positive guidance helps preschoolers make progress in being able to wait for a turn, share a favorite toy, solve problems, make plans, and engage in cooperative play. Teachers help preschoolers recognize strong feelings—their own and those of other children and adults—and respond in ways that the group understands and accepts.

Foundations Underlying Quality

How might a visitor to a preschool classroom recognize the use of positive guidance strategies that help children learn how to regulate their behavior? What are the signs that children are learning to recognize, name, and manage strong feelings? Positive guidance for preschoolers reflects the following beliefs and actions:

☀ Preschoolers are at their own unique stage of development. They are neither a bigger version of toddlers nor a smaller version of school-age children. They are active learners whose skills are expanding in all areas of development and who are mastering new content areas and gaining a foundation for the academic learning they will pursue in elementary school.

☀ Preschoolers are at a developmental stage where their ability to empathize is growing. Many preschoolers now realize that other people have feelings and desires and are learning to adjust their behavior accordingly. They make friends and are eager to please adults. Effective teachers help preschoolers form and maintain friendships.

☀ Preschoolers can and will learn from positive guidance strategies. They can understand why rules are necessary and are able to take personal responsibility for their own well-being and respect the well-being of others.

☀ Preschoolers have the cognitive and language skills needed to recognize and talk about their feelings and help identify the reasons for their behavior—whether appropriate or inappropriate. When inappropriate behavior is ongoing and harmful to the child or to others, teachers and families work together to help the child learn new ways to get needs met.

What Positive Guidance Should Look Like

In a preschool room, teachers use a variety of individualized positive guidance strategies to prevent unsafe behaviors and encourage development and learning. They calmly remind children of rules and guidelines, offer choices and opportunities to express ideas and contribute to planning, and accept the unique characteristics of this age group. In the following examples, you will see what strategies and outcomes should be in place when you visit a preschool program and why these are important.

What you should see	Why
A safe, well-planned, and developmentally appropriate environment that supports preschoolers, teachers, and their families.	Creating an environment that reflects preschoolers' current stages of development, cultures, home languages, families, and interests will prevent most problem behaviors that result from unrealistic expectations for the age group.
Teachers invite children to help establish a few important rules that are stated in a positive way—telling children what they should do instead of what they should not do.	Children are more likely to understand and remember rules when they take part in establishing them. Positive statements tell children what to do, making them easier to remember.
Teachers acknowledge children's strong feelings, while guiding them to express those feelings through words or to cope with them through another outlet, such as art, physical activity, or listening to music. For example, "I think you are frustrated because you want to pull the wagon. Ask Janis, 'Can I please have a turn?'"	Preschoolers have strong feelings; they may bring them to the program or take them home after a challenging day. Teachers can help preschoolers recognize and name their feelings—a first step in coping with feelings in positive ways that do not harm other people or things.
Teachers describe desired actions in positive terms that tell children what is expected. For example, "Put on the safety goggles before you start hammering. Your eyes will be protected from wood splinters."	When teachers provide a clear statement of what children can do as well as what behavior is not acceptable, children learn what is expected of them and are more likely to comply with the request.
Teachers introduce a simple, step-by-step conflict resolution process and remind children to use it when disagreements arise. Children discuss and resolve their conflicts on their own or with the teacher's support when necessary.	Disagreements occur in almost all preschool settings. Preschoolers have lots of ideas, and they don't always go along with what their peers want to do. Teachers can help children develop social skills, such as cooperation, negotiation, and problem solving, by teaching them a simple process they can use to discuss and develop solutions on their own. Children can ask the teacher for help if they find themselves unable to agree on a solution.

What you should see	Why
Teachers provide many opportunities for preschoolers to make choices throughout the day.	Preschoolers are eager to make decisions for themselves, but they need practice in making appropriate decisions. Teachers can offer acceptable choices at snacktimes and mealtimes, in interest areas, when selecting a book to read, when choosing partners for a movement activity, and when selecting art media and tools to explore.
Teachers include children in doing meaningful tasks that keep the environment safe and tidy.	Preschoolers want to be like adults and perform grown-up activities. Effective teachers provide child-size tools and invite children to take part in tasks such as sweeping and vacuuming, and clearing, setting, and wiping tables. When children feel like a part of their community, they feel important and valued. They are more likely to comply with rules and use positive behavior.
Teachers stop or adjust what they are doing to address the needs of a child who is distressed.	Schedules and plans need to be as flexible as preschoolers are unpredictable. When a child is upset and needs immediate attention, one of the teachers should respond. A calm and quick response often prevents a behavior from escalating and getting out of hand.
Once a child is no longer acting out or using a problem behavior and has regained self-control, teachers have a private discussion with the child.	Preschoolers have strong emotions and often cannot talk about their behavior in the moment. They are more likely to be able to discuss the reasons for an outburst or aggressive action once they are calm. At this point, they can also listen and, with the teacher's assistance, plan different ways to behave in the future.
Teachers consider the reasons why a child might be losing control, using aggression, or acting out in other ways.	There is a reason and purpose for all behavior. A child might act out to ask for attention, to express a desire or frustration, or because he is feeling overwhelmed by stress or just tired of spending time in the group. Helping a child learn how to cope with feelings in positive ways begins with figuring out the reasons for the behavior.

What you should see	Why
Teachers involve families in helping children replace a challenging behavior with one that meets their need but is appropriate.	Teachers and families together can plan an approach and consistent strategies to use at home and at the program. When the plan is implemented in a caring way, the child can learn new ways to express feelings and make requests for attention.
Teachers help children who use bullying behaviors as well as children who are the target of bullies.	It's important to identify the reason for the bullying and teach the children different ways to address the root cause. This should be addressed as soon as possible so the bullying behaviors do not become a pattern that carries into future years. It's equally important to pay attention to children who are the target, giving them suggestions of what to say and do when bullying behaviors are directed at them.

When you observe the twelve items noted above in place, it is likely that your program's positive guidance strategies are serving preschoolers well. Use the checklist in appendix D to observe how well your program meets these criteria. For items that your program is not yet addressing well, work with teachers to devise and implement an action plan for improvement. As a supervisor, you are responsible for ensuring that positive guidance supports children's growth, development, and learning.

When Guidance Strategies Need Further Adjusting

For deeper insight into the effectiveness of the program's positive guidance approach, it's important to observe preschoolers and their teachers. Knowledge of positive guidance strategies does not always translate into their effective use. If you spot warning signs such as those in the examples described below, it's time to look more closely and try to identify what might be causing the situation. Discuss the possible solutions noted in the third column with teachers and help them better understand how the use of positive guidance is a teaching strategy that helps children learn how to behave in acceptable ways.

Note: Some of the warning signs listed below may be caused by factors other than inappropriate guidance strategies or by a combination of inappropriate guidance strategies and other factors. Regular observations will provide information about the precise cause of the problem.

Warning sign	Why this might be happening	How educators can address the problem
Teachers place children in a time-out chair if they break rules or lose control.	Teachers see this as an acceptable alternative to physical punishment and have few other strategies to employ in guiding children's behavior. They may not know that to the child, time-out is a punishment and does not teach positive behavior.	Review the definitions of punishment, guidance, discipline, and self-regulation and the program's positive guidance policies. Have teachers discuss the results of using time-outs. For example, ask, "Does time-out teach children to control their impulses, express their feelings, or regulate their behavior?" Help teachers become skilled in using a variety of positive guidance strategies that can be individualized to address the needs of different children.
Teachers frequently correct children and belittle them for forgetting the rules or not knowing how to respond to a request.	Teachers may believe that these approaches to guiding children's behavior are effective. They do not know that many times children do not know what adults are asking them to do because adults have not clearly described the desired behavior.	First, make sure teachers know that correcting and belittling children are not permitted, and use of positive guidance is required. Next, discuss how there are many things we ask of children that they do not know how to do. For example, they may not know the steps in hand washing until we tell them. Explain that children need step-by-step instructions for some tasks.
Teachers focus on children's challenging behavior without looking for and addressing the causes for the behavior.	Teachers may not understand there is a reason for all behavior. Helping children learn alternate ways to get their needs met begins with identifying when and why the behavior is used.	Work with teachers to define challenging behaviors and use an individualized plan to address the cause of a challenging behavior and help the child learn more appropriate ways to handle strong feelings. At the same time, underscore the need for the teacher to work with families so their children can learn to use alternative behaviors to cope with strong feelings at home and at the program.
Teachers shout to colleagues and to children from one side of the room to the other.	Teachers may not realize that some preschoolers are scared when they hear a loud voice. Shouting does not make it easier for the child to hear the message. Some teachers just don't realize how loud their voices are.	Discuss how most people feel—both children and adults—when someone shouts at them. Ask teachers to commit to using normal voice levels and to get down to children's eye level when speaking with children.

Warning sign	Why this might be happening	How educators can address the problem
Teachers expect children to behave in ways that do not match their stage of development and admonish children for not conforming. For example, they have children sit for long periods of time or require the whole group to do the same activity at the same time.	Teachers may not understand that while there are many things preschoolers can do, there are many other things they are still learning or are not developmentally ready to learn. They may think they are preparing children for kindergarten.	Review a planned activity that is developmentally inappropriate and help teachers revise it in a way that is appropriate for the children's ages, abilities, and cultures. For example, instead of lecturing the whole group about how to write numerals, the teachers could provide a variety of math-related materials for children to explore in the math and manipulatives center.
Teachers complain and reprimand children for taking things from one interest center to use in another.	Teachers may not view a child as being thoughtful and creative when she carries the cardboard blocks to the housekeeping corner to make a couch. They may think it is more important to keep things tidy and in their place.	Help teachers step back and see such activities from the child's perspective. In this example, the house area has no couch, so the child saw the perfect materials for making one in the block area and used them accordingly. Explain that while materials may be stored in one area, it's okay to move them to another area to enhance children's play and activities.
Teachers share news of a child's typical but not positive behavior with families at the end of the day rather than sharing the wonderful things their child did and learned.	Teachers think that parents want to know what their child did "wrong." They do not realize that pickup time is not an appropriate time to raise something that may or may not be a long-term issue.	Encourage teachers to recognize the stressors present at pickup time as children and families reunite after being apart for the day. Explain that it is more appropriate to talk about a problem behavior at a time when a full discussion can take place. Pickup time is for sharing good news.
Teachers frequently remind children to follow specific rules.	Over time, the number of rules can get out of hand. There may be so many that no one can remember where they came from or what purpose they serve. It is likely that rules established for a previous group situation are not necessary.	Ask teachers to list the rules, their purpose, and the desired behaviors. Have them analyze the list to see which rules can be eliminated and which can be combined. For example, the rule "Keep your hands to yourself" is likely covered by "Be nice to others."

5 Engaging Families

High-quality early childhood programs value and actively promote shared, meaningful partnerships with children's families. "Family engagement occurs when there is an on-going, reciprocal, strengths-based partnership between families and their children's early childhood education programs" (Halgunseth et al. 2009, 3). Although family engagement is important with children at every age, the younger the child, the more critical it is for programs to foster trusting and respectful relationships between staff and families. The ongoing exchange of information with a child's family provides insights into the child's unique characteristics, strengths, needs, and interests. In situations in which the teacher's culture and home language differ from that of a child and family, families are the best resource for learning about the expectations and communication patterns that influence how the child relates to others and interprets experiences. Family engagement should be individualized—tailored to reflect each family's unique goals, interests, and characteristics.

Note: In this chapter, we alternate use of *family* and *parent* to signify the person or persons who have primary responsibility for the child's well-being or who play a significant role in the child's upbringing.

Foundations Underlying Quality

A report from NAEYC (accessed 2017), *Principles of Effective Practice*, describes six principles of family engagement. These include the following:

1. **"Programs invite families to participate in decision making and goal setting for their child."**
   This takes place in formal and informal discussions and contexts. For example, at the end of a day, a parent might mention to the teacher that the child's pediatrician suggests it's time to start her baby on solid foods. At a formal conference, the teacher and family would review all of the new foods the baby has tried and plan for what to introduce in the future.

2. **"Teachers and programs engage families in two-way communication."**
Whether through in-person chats, e-mail messages, texts, video calls (through FaceTime, Skype, or other apps), or phone calls, teachers and families exchange information that can be applied to better support the child.

3. **"Programs and teachers engage families in ways that are truly reciprocal."**
Teachers use what they learn from families in the classroom, and families use what they learn from teachers to support their child at home. For example, families and teachers confer about the most effective way to help a toddler who shows signs she is ready for toilet learning.

4. **"Programs provide learning activities for the home and in the community."**
For example, teachers create reading backpacks with children's books and activities to use at home. Families can borrow them for a week and then return them to the program to allow the next family to enjoy them. The program celebrates the NAEYC event Week of the Young Child by setting up a reading center at a mall and distributing information about reading aloud.

5. **"Programs invite families to participate in program-level decisions and wider advocacy efforts."**
The program establishes a parent council to advise on large purchases, curriculum changes, and advising policy makers and funders on issues important to families and young children. For example, a group might invite a state legislator to tour the program to garner support for early childhood education.

6. **"Programs implement a comprehensive program-level system."**
Teachers and other staff work with families to create and implement family engagement strategies and practices for the entire program. For example, this group schedules a program-wide cleanup day or children's used book swap.

What Family Engagement Should Look Like

To engage families in the program in meaningful ways, teachers must appreciate the value of family engagement and know how to achieve it. Listed below are some examples of strategies that promote mutually respectful partnerships with families and why these strategies are important.

What you should see	Why
Teachers provide an orientation to the program for children and families at the start of the year and as needed when new families enroll during the year; orientation takes place at an open house or through home visits at the beginning of the year and again during the year. Families receive a written guide to the program, provided in their home language.	A program orientation is the first step in developing a meaningful, joint relationship with families. It is a time for teachers to get to know the child and family and to explain the program philosophy, key policies, and practices. In addition, the orientation gives families an opportunity to meet and begin getting to know the person who will care for and teach their child and to share their goals for their child.
Teachers greet family members by name at pickup and drop-off times; teachers correctly pronounce everyone's name.	Families are more likely to feel accepted and valued when they have a personal relationship with the adults who teach their children during the day. Pronouncing names correctly is a sign of respect. The children benefit too, as they see their teacher and parents warmly engaged with each other.
Teachers and families exchange information about the child, such as a brief anecdote, news about the morning's routines, something the child needs, or a child's special interest or new skill. Teachers and families use a system for regularly communicating with each other about the program and about each child.	Effective partnerships rely on information shared frequently and accurately. Families want and need to know about their child's life at the program, and teachers need and want to know about the child's life at home. Experiences in both settings contribute to the child's growth, development, and learning. For infants and toddlers, daily communication about routines reassures families that they are actively involved in their children's care. For older children, an end-of-the-week summary works well, augmented by updates as needed.
Teachers provide news and updates about the children's activities on a regular schedule and through multiple venues such as individual journals and mailboxes, a family bulletin board, website, or a paper or digital newsletter; they include the weekly schedule, current menus, upcoming program events, community notices, and photographs of children engaged in activities. Written communications are in all languages used by families in the program.	Families feel empowered by knowing what is going on at the program—and can read this information in their home language. They are more likely to become engaged if they can read about and see pictures of their children's daily life. Some parents consume information on-site, while others prefer to visit the program's website once they have finished their evening routines.
Families stop by a designated area filled with pamphlets, articles, and other resources of interest to parents of young children; a comfortable nursing area is available in the infant room.	Including a special place for family members conveys the message that their needs are considered important and that resources are available to help them. Providing a place for a mother to nurse an infant before leaving or when dropping by during the day is an excellent way to support the child and mother.

What you should see	Why
Teachers encourage family members to participate in the program by sharing a skill or interest or some aspect of their home language and culture.	Family members have a lot to contribute to enrich the children's experiences. Inviting them to share their knowledge and skills conveys respect and provides a way for them to enhance the curriculum for all of the children in the group. Children take pride in seeing their family members visit and take part in the program.
Teachers, other staff, and family volunteers plan meetings and workshops focused on topics of interest to families, giving them an opportunity to hear guest speakers and to learn about the program.	Family members will be most interested in attending meetings and workshops that are of interest to them as parents. What was of interest to last year's families might or might not be of interest to the families in attendance this year, so the program should conduct an annual survey of family interests. In-person events offer a venue for learning and for getting to know other members of the community.
Teachers and families take part in regular conferences at the program, in the community, or during home visits, sharing information, reviewing the child's progress, and planning ways to support the child at home and at the program in the future; teachers share documentation of the child's activities through multiple sources, including photos, work samples, and assessment results.	Regularly scheduled conferences allow families and teachers to review the child's progress in all domains in an organized way. Joint planning ensures that the family and teacher agree on appropriate ways to support the child's continued learning.
Teachers and families plan and participate in program-wide events, such as a movie night or preparing the garden for the spring planting; such events involve children, parents, and staff in enjoyable activities.	Relationships between children and family members are supported when they have opportunities to have fun together. Teachers learn more about children when they can see them interacting with their families.
Older toddlers and preschoolers eagerly show their families photos and examples of their work displayed in the classroom; the children are excited to tell their families what they did and learned.	Families can learn about their child's experiences from teachers and from the child. Revisiting an experience supports the child's learning and reinforces the bond between parent and child.
Teachers provide an orientation and resources, such as tip sheets for family members who are classroom volunteers; they ask family members what they would be comfortable doing with the children.	Parents and other family members are the experts on their own children, but they may need information and guidance when other children are involved. For example, they may be great at reading to one child but unsure of what strategies work when reading to a group. Everyone will have a better experience if teachers offer the volunteer information about best practices for the age group.

What you should see	Why
Teachers welcome family members to visit the classroom at any time during the day; family members do not need to have an appointment to drop in.	Families are as much a part of the program as children and teachers. They should be welcomed whenever they have time to visit—to share a snack or meal, to pick up a child for a medical appointment, or to observe their child at play. In some programs, open access is considered a way to ensure families that the program is dedicated to prevention of child maltreatment.

When you observe the twelve items noted above in place, it is likely that your program is effectively engaging families. Use the checklist in appendix E to observe how well your program meets these criteria. For items that your program is not yet addressing well, work with teachers to devise and implement an action plan for improvement. As a supervisor, you are responsible for ensuring family engagement strategies are effective in developing teacher-family partnerships that support children's growth, development, and learning.

When Family Engagement Strategies Need Further Adjusting

Assessing the effectiveness of family engagement requires more than a visit to the program. Some of the indicators are subtle and take time to uncover. If you note any of the warning signs listed below, teachers may need your support and encouragement to successfully engage families in the program. Discuss the possible solutions in the third column with teachers and help them better understand how family engagement supports everyone.

Note: Some of the warning signs listed below may be caused by factors other than family engagement problems or by a combination of family engagement problems and other factors. Regular observations will provide information about the precise cause of the problem.

Warning sign	Why this might be happening	How educators can address the problem
Families complain that their children are not challenged by the curriculum and that the program is not preparing them to be successful in school and in life.	Teachers may not know how to explain what children of a given age are learning through the curriculum or why the materials, activities, and experiences are appropriate for the children's stage of development.	Work with teachers to develop a handout or online resource for families on what children are learning and how it is connected to the academic learning that will take place in the elementary grades. Ask teachers to share the questions they are asked so they can collectively answer them through this resource. Include summaries of research that focus on the long-term benefits of developmentally appropriate practice. Invite an expert on developmentally appropriate practice to provide a workshop for families.

Warning sign	Why this might be happening	How educators can address the problem
Family members see teachers as experts in child development and feel that parents should have no role in their child's experiences at the program.	This feeling can be the result of a parent's own experiences in school, where family engagement was not emphasized. Perhaps the family holds a cultural value that views teachers as the only authorities on educating young children. Or the family could be too busy to play a role and feel that it is the teacher's job to educate their child.	Work with teachers and families to plan and conduct an event that gives families and children a chance to experience typical activities together. For example, in the infant room, parents and babies can roll a ball back and forth; in the toddler room, parents and toddlers can march with rhythm instruments; and in the preschool room, parents and children can build block structures. Remind teachers to frequently ask families for input about supporting their child's development and to share with families how they used their suggestions and how their child responded. This strategy will let parents know that the program values their input on decisions involving their children.
Families drop off and pick up their children without talking with teachers. They leave the classroom as quickly as possible.	Teachers may inadvertently give the message that they do not have time for or interest in talking with families. Or they may have conveyed that these transition times should be brief so children do not get upset.	Observe drop-off and pickup transition times to gather information and to model greeting and sharing information with parents. Help teachers understand the significance of separation for children of different ages and for their families. Teachers and families can work together to plan individualized strategies that ease the transition. Also, review how important it is for children to see their teachers and family members talking and sharing the joy in children's activities and progress.
Information provided through bulletin boards, newsletters, the website, or other announcements for families is out of date.	Teachers may be so caught up in their daily planning for children that they are not focused on sharing information with families. They may feel that their daily interactions with families are sufficient for keeping them informed. They may need to establish a schedule for updating the information shared with families.	Have teachers develop a schedule for providing regular updates. Suggest they seek a parent volunteer who can assist if time is an issue. Ask them to consider how families value regular communication and news updates.

Warning sign	Why this might be happening	How educators can address the problem
Family workshops and meetings have poor attendance; teachers state that parents are not interested in these events.	Many families of young children find it impossible to attend evening meetings due to work or other responsibilities; some families cannot afford to pay others to care for their children; or the topics addressed at these events are not of interest to families.	Work with teachers to review the process—typically a questionnaire—used to assess families' interests in the topics addressed through meetings and workshops. Update the approach as needed to make sure current interests and needs are being addressed. Offer potluck meals at the end of the day or on weekends. Provide child care if that is the deterrent to attendance. Suggest that teachers enlist the help of engaged family members to revamp these events to better address the needs of families who currently attend the program.
Family-teacher conferences and home visits take place only when there is a problem that requires in-depth discussion and planning.	Family-teacher conferences are not a part of the program's annual schedule, so they are not a regular occurrence. Teachers may think that their daily or weekly communications with families are sufficient. Teachers may not know how to conduct conferences or fear that the families will criticize them.	Discuss the issue with teachers and other staff to find out why conferences are not part of the regular schedule. If needed, alter the schedule to include conferences three times a year. Provide resources about the differences between conferences and informal communications and how to plan and conduct conferences.
Typically only mothers and female family members are engaged with the program; fathers and male family members do not participate.	Early childhood programs have many more female than male teachers and other staff. As a result, male family members may feel out of place in the setting. It takes a conscious effort to plan ways to welcome and engage fathers and other male family members in the program. Perhaps the program has not addressed this issue yet.	Work with teachers to create and administer a family survey that suggests a variety of ways for all adults to become engaged with the program and children's development and learning. Review the results and ask for volunteers to form a group to focus on gender-neutral family engagement strategies. This group can research what has worked well for other early childhood programs. They might consult online resources, such as https://eclkc.ohs.acf.hhs.gov/sites/default/files/pdf/father-engage-programming.pdf or www.naeyc.org/files/tyc/file/InvolvingFathers.pdf.
Teachers gossip and discuss a child's behavior with the family members of other children.	Teachers may have developed such a relaxed relationship with a family that they may not realize they have stepped over the line and are being unprofessional. Sometimes teachers live in the same community as the families and have not developed boundaries for the kinds of conversations that are appropriate and those that are not appropriate.	Hold a workshop or provide resources on confidentiality and why teachers must maintain confidentiality when talking with families. Explain that it is never appropriate to discuss a child's behavior with another person unless that person is the child's parents or a staff member with a "need to know." In those instances, such conversations should be private and held at a time when both teacher and parent are available for a full discussion. Remind teachers that gossiping is never acceptable and those taking part are harming their colleagues, the children, and the families.

When families are engaged with the program, everyone benefits. Families have meaningful ways to participate as part of a team and to contribute to their child's daily routines and activities. The more families learn about the program and its goals for their children, the more they can extend and reinforce learning and development at home. Teachers can be more effective when families share insights about their children and contribute time and resources to enrich the curriculum. And children benefit the most when the significant adults in their lives work together to give them the support and guidance they need to grow and develop. Children establish trust more easily when they see that their worlds are closely linked.

Appendix A

Checklist for Maintaining Healthy and Safe Environments for Young Children

This checklist is intended to be a guide for supervisors in assessing your program's compliance with standards for safe and healthy indoor and outdoor environments. Please be aware that your program/school/setting may also be subject to requirements set by funders and the federal, state, or local governments. You will need to consider those regulations first when assessing your program.

As you go through this checklist, you will note that it contains items relevant to programs and schools serving infants, toddlers, and preschoolers. As such, some items may not pertain to the setting you supervise. Mark those items that are not relevant as N/A (not applicable). Work with teachers to complete the checklist.

1. Health and Safety in the Indoor Environment

OVERALL

Standard	Met	Not met	Date	Notes
1. The environment is smoke-free, lead-free, and toxin-free (including plants).				
2. The air temperature is 68–70°F. (In dry climates, a humidifier is used to moisten the air.)				
3. Water temperature is 120°F or less.				
4. Smoke alarms and carbon monoxide detectors (if required) are in place and tested according to fire code.				
5. A-B-C type fire extinguishers are charged, easy to access, and stored in visible locations. Operating instructions are posted in English and the home languages of staff and families.				
6. Emergency exits are marked, lit, and unlocked from the inside.				
7. Up-to-date emergency numbers for poison control, fire, police, and medical assistance are prominently posted.				
8. Diagrammed evacuation procedures are clearly posted with instructions in English and in the home languages of staff and families.				
9. Emergency lighting, including flashlights with working batteries, are available in case of power failure.				
10. A fully stocked first-aid kit is stored in a locked cabinet, out of children's reach.				
11. A working telephone is accessible and charged.				
12. Chemicals and potentially dangerous products such as cleaning supplies, bleach, and medications are stored in original, labeled containers in a locked cabinet that is not accessible to children.				
13. Sinks, liquid soap, and disposable paper towels are available to staff and children at all times.				
14. Bathroom surfaces, sinks, faucets, countertops, toilets, diaper pails, and potty chairs are cleaned and sanitized daily with freshly made bleach solution or another approved product.				

Adapted from *Essentials for Working with Young Children*, Second Edition, edited by Valora Washington. 2017. Washington, DC: Council for Professional Recognition. Reused with permission in *High-Quality Early Childhood Programs: The What, Why, and How* by Laura J. Colker and Derry Koralek, © 2018. Published by Redleaf Press, www.redleafpress.org. This page may be reproduced for individual or classroom use only.

EQUIPMENT AND MATERIALS

Standard	Met	Not met	Date	Notes
1. Crib slats are no more than 2⅜ inches apart.				
2. Cribs are positioned near exits in case of emergency.				
3. Cribs have no mirrors, mobiles, or hanging toys.				
4. Cribs are cleaned and sanitized after each use.				
5. Toddler and preschool mats/cots are spaced at least three feet apart during rest time to prevent the spread of germs.				
6. Toddler and preschool mats/cots are stored out of the way in racks from bottom to top so they will not topple over.				
7. Area rugs are vacuumed or shaken outside daily and laundered weekly.				
8. Mats and rugs lie flat and pose no tripping hazards.				
9. Window blinds and/or shades have plastic rods instead of cords.				
10. Pets are permitted according to governing regulations and housed away from food preparation and eating areas.				
11. Pet food and litter are stored out of children's reach. Only adults clean pet habitats.				
12. Electrical outlets are covered with child-resistant caps when not in use.				
13. Electrical cords are not frayed or damaged.				
14. Electrical cords and wires are tied together, on top of the floor covering, and located in low-traffic areas, away from water.				
15. Toys and equipment have no sharp edges, chipped paint, lead paint, or loose nuts and bolts.				

Standard	Met	Not met	Date	Notes
16. Toy pieces and removable parts are larger than 1¼ inches in diameter.				
17. Balls are larger than 1¾ inches in diameter.				
18. The setting has no safety pins, small jewelry, coins, button-type batteries, Styrofoam objects, or marbles.				
19. Play equipment and materials are designed to allow all children in the group to participate and are adapted to address particular special needs.				

Adapted from *Essentials for Working with Young Children*, Second Edition, edited by Valora Washington. 2017. Washington, DC: Council for Professional Recognition. Reused with permission in *High-Quality Early Childhood Programs: The What, Why, and How* by Laura J. Colker and Derry Koralek, © 2018. Published by Redleaf Press, www.redleafpress.org. This page may be reproduced for individual or classroom use only.

2. Health and Safety in the Outdoor Environment

OVERALL

Standard	Met	Not met	Date	Notes
1. The environment is smoke-free, lead-free, and toxin-free (including plants).				
2. The area is free of holes, tripping hazards, and debris, including glass, standing water, ice, and animal wastes.				
3. The area is enclosed by a natural barrier or a fence at least 4 feet high. The fence openings are no larger than 3½ inches and free of splinters and sharp edges.				
4. Exit gates have self-closing, child-proof latches.				
5. The ground and sandbox allow for drainage.				
6. The area has no trampolines, teeter-totters, belt swings, single-chain tire swings, or enclosed tunnel slides.				
7. Pets kept outdoors are permitted by governing regulations.				
8. Pet food and litter are stored out of children's reach. Only adults clean pet habitats.				
9. The sandbox is raked before use and covered when not in use to prevent animals from using it as a litter box.				
10. Children wear helmets while using tricycles and other riding toys. If helmets are shared, the helmet lining is wiped clean with a damp cloth after each use to remove any lice, nits, or fungal spores.				
11. Storage sheds are locked.				
12. A first-aid kit and charged cell phone are accessible.				

Adapted from *Essentials for Working with Young Children*, Second Edition, edited by Valora Washington. 2017. Washington, DC: Council for Professional Recognition. Reused with permission in *High-Quality Early Childhood Programs: The What, Why, and How* by Laura J. Colker and Derry Koralek, © 2018. Published by Redleaf Press, www.redleafpress.org. This page may be reproduced for individual or classroom use only.

INSTALLED EQUIPMENT AND STRUCTURES

Standard	Met	Not met	Date	Notes
1. Play structures 30 inches or lower in height are at least 6 feet apart; taller play structures are at least 9 feet apart.				
2. Play structures are securely anchored to the ground and free of sharp edges, rust, rot, cracks, peeling paint, and protruding nails and bolts.				
3. Elevated surfaces such as platforms have guardrails.				
4. Infant swings are fully enclosed and have seat belts.				
5. Toddler swings are "bucket-shaped."				
6. Infant and toddler swings have a 48-inch fall zone.				
7. Preschool swings have a single axis (known as to-fro) and S-hooks used in suspension are closed completely.				
8. Preschool swings are suspended a minimum of 12 inches off the ground.				
9. Preschool swings and play equipment have a 6-foot fall zone.				
10. Cushioning material such as wood chips, mulch, or sand is under and around play equipment, according to the depth specified for each type of equipment by the US Consumer Product Safety Commission (an average of 10–12 inches).				
11. Climbers are no more than 60 inches high.				
12. Play equipment and surfaces accommodate children with special needs, including those who use walkers and wheelchairs				

Adapted from *Essentials for Working with Young Children*, Second Edition, edited by Valora Washington. 2017. Washington, DC: Council for Professional Recognition. Reused with permission in *High-Quality Early Childhood Programs: The What, Why, and How* by Laura J. Colker and Derry Koralek, © 2018. Published by Redleaf Press, www.redleafpress.org. This page may be reproduced for individual or classroom use only.

Appendix B

Observation Checklists for Ensuring Quality in Infant Programs

As you complete these checklists, you may wish to take notes regarding the status of the characteristics you observe. Add the dates of your observations if that information will be helpful to you.

1. Infant Environment Observation Checklist

Environmental characteristic	Observed		
	Yes	Somewhat	Not yet
1. Cozy, homelike touches and items specific to the children's cultures and home languages.			
2. Safety mirrors and photos of enrolled infants and their families displayed at children's eye level.			
3. Soft (carpeted), protected areas in the indoor environment for children to sit, creep, crawl, walk, and push wheeled toys and cars.			
4. Areas with easy-to-clean flooring where messy activities take place.			
5. An inviting family greeting space where teachers welcome children and families and exchange information about the children.			
6. An easily sanitized diapering area well stocked with supplies and a foot-operated trash can lined with a plastic bag.			
7. Cribs for each child located in an open area where they are visible to teachers.			
8. Comfortable adult-size chairs or gliders available in a private spot for nursing mothers and teachers to bottle-feed infants.			
9. Sturdy furniture and equipment that infants can use indoors and outdoors to pull themselves up.			
10. Culturally and developmentally appropriate toys and other learning materials displayed on low, open shelving.			
11. Outdoor play space for infants adjacent to but separate from where toddlers play. The space for young infants is protected from older, mobile children.			
12. Storage spaces and furniture available for adults.			

From *High-Quality Early Childhood Programs: The What, Why, and How* by Laura J. Colker and Derry Koralek, © 2018. Published by Redleaf Press, www.redleafpress.org. This page may be reproduced for individual or classroom use only.

2. Infant Toys, Materials, and Equipment Observation Checklist

Toys, materials, and equipment characteristic	Observed		
	Yes	Somewhat	Not yet
1. Items available that infants can explore with all of their senses.			
2. Toys and other available materials have bright colors, interesting shapes, and noisy parts.			
3. Items available indoors encourage mobile infants to move and gain gross-motor and fine-motor skills.			
4. Household items available for use in play.			
5. Open-ended toys, materials, and equipment available for play.			
6. Natural materials available for infants to explore and manipulate.			
7. Materials available that encourage pretending and taking on roles.			
8. Washable books with simple pictures of familiar things, repetitive language, rhymes, or no words, in English and home languages, available to children.			
9. Materials available that encourage problem solving and other cognitive skills.			
10. Materials available that promote the visual arts and music.			
11. Unbreakable, child-size plates, bowls, cups, forks, and spoons available to mobile infants for meals.			
12. Equipment and materials available outdoors that promote gross-motor activity and interaction with nature.			

From *High-Quality Early Childhood Programs: The What, Why, and How* by Laura J. Colker and Derry Koralek, © 2018. Published by Redleaf Press, www.redleafpress.org. This page may be reproduced for individual or classroom use only.

3. Infant Program Structure Observation Checklist

Program structure characteristic	Observed		
	Yes	Somewhat	Not yet
1. Teachers and infants follow a flexible schedule of simple and consistent routines that are tailored to meet the needs of individual children.			
2. Activities are scheduled between routines.			
3. Teachers follow infants' cues as to when a routine or activity begins and ends.			
4. Teachers take advantage of "teachable moments."			
5. Family members and teachers exchange information about an infant's day or evening, progress in gaining skills, and just to touch base.			
6. Teachers take infants outside daily.			
7. Infants play with one or two other children during the day.			
8. Teachers talk to and interact with infants in a relaxed manner during repeated routines.			
9. Mobile infants actively participate in routines, doing as much as they can for themselves.			
10. Teachers take infants from their cribs as soon as they notice the child is awake.			
11. Mobile infants eat lunch together at child-size tables with two to three other children.			
12. Teachers invite mobile infants to get out of their chairs after eating and move on to another activity.			

From *High-Quality Early Childhood Programs: The What, Why, and How* by Laura J. Colker and Derry Koralek, © 2018. Published by Redleaf Press, www.redleafpress.org. This page may be reproduced for individual or classroom use only.

4. Infant Curriculum Observation Checklist

Curriculum characteristic	Observed		
	Yes	Somewhat	Not yet
1. Teachers promptly respond when infants communicate through verbal and nonverbal cues that they are tired, are hungry, or need a clean and dry diaper.			
2. Teachers introduce and reinforce skills based on what they observe children doing and learning.			
3. Teachers use routines as opportunities to promote learning.			
4. Children play with toys and materials they have selected for themselves.			
5. Teachers regularly observe children's interactions and activities, document what they see and hear, and maintain individual portfolios.			
6. Children use their large muscles in various activities throughout the day.			
7. Children use the small muscles in their hands in various activities throughout the day.			
8. Teachers engage both verbal and nonverbal infants in conversation during the day's routines and activities.			
9. Children solve problems, explore cause and effect, and apply old knowledge to new situations throughout the day.			
10. Children express themselves through the creative arts each day.			
11. Teachers ensure that the curriculum is accessible to all children, including those with special needs.			
12. Family members share their skills and interests and play with, read to, and otherwise engage the children.			

From *High-Quality Early Childhood Programs: The What, Why, and How* by Laura J. Colker and Derry Koralek, © 2018. Published by Redleaf Press, www.redleafpress.org. This page may be reproduced for individual or classroom use only.

5. Infant Supportive Interactions Observation Checklist

Supportive interaction characteristic	Observed		
	Yes	Somewhat	Not yet
1. Teachers sit on the floor with infants reading books, singing songs, talking, and playing with toys.			
2. Teachers comfort a child who is frightened when a new person enters the room.			
3. Teachers show pleasure and encouragement when a child attempts and achieves a goal.			
4. Teachers respond to infants' cries, gestures, coos, gurgles, and first words by interpreting the communication and talking back to the child.			
5. Teachers encourage mobile infants' use of self-help skills as soon as they are developmentally ready to do so.			
6. Teachers accept spills and messes as a natural part of learning for mobile infants.			
7. Teachers give attention to several infants at the same time.			
8. Teachers model pretend behaviors and join in children's pretend play.			
9. Teachers use information shared by a child's family when talking with the child.			
10. Teachers vary tone of voice, nonverbal responses, and interactions to fit an infant's temperament.			
11. Teachers learn and use a few important words and phrases in the child's home language.			
12. Mobile infants begin to play alongside each other and show beginning signs of empathy.			

From *High-Quality Early Childhood Programs: The What, Why, and How* by Laura J. Colker and Derry Koralek, © 2018. Published by Redleaf Press, www.redleafpress.org. This page may be reproduced for individual or classroom use only.

6. Infant Positive Guidance Observation Checklist

Positive guidance characteristic	Observed		
	Yes	Somewhat	Not yet
1. A safe, well-planned, and developmentally appropriate environment that supports adults and infants.			
2. Teachers respond consistently and promptly to infants who are crying; teachers hold and cuddle infants until they have calmed.			
3. Teachers hold young infants close, look at their faces, smile, and talk; infants respond with coos and gurgles.			
4. Teachers redirect babies from potentially frustrating or dangerous situations by physically moving them or offering an interesting play material.			
5. Teachers wait to see whether infants can solve problems on their own before stepping in to help.			
6. Teachers offer interesting alternatives when two children want to play with the same toy.			
7. Teachers model caring behaviors, such as stroking hair instead of pulling it.			
8. Teachers say no only when necessary to keep a child safe.			
9. Teachers frequently offer choices to older infants and then accept children's decisions.			
10. Teachers acknowledge infants' communications and activities using names and verbal and nonverbal responses.			
11. Teachers invite mobile infants to help do real jobs.			
12. Teachers demonstrate respect for children's families and cultures.			

From *High-Quality Early Childhood Programs: The What, Why, and How* by Laura J. Colker and Derry Koralek, © 2018. Published by Redleaf Press, www.redleafpress.org. This page may be reproduced for individual or classroom use only.

Appendix C

Observation Checklists for Ensuring Quality in Toddler Programs

As you complete these checklists, you may wish to take notes regarding the status of the characteristics you observe. Add the dates of your observations if that information will be helpful to you.

1. Toddler Environment Observation Checklist

Environmental characteristic	Observed		
	Yes	Somewhat	Not yet
1. A welcome area where families talk with teachers, get information about their children and the program, and find parenting resources.			
2. Photographs of the children prominently displayed in cubbies and throughout the classroom.			
3. Materials and displays represent the children's home languages, cultures, and family structures.			
4. Furnishings, flooring textures, tape, and exits clearly define interest areas and manage traffic flow.			
5. Messy activities take place on washable flooring, while other activities occur on carpeted floors.			
6. Materials displayed on low shelving labeled with pictures and words in both English and home languages.			
7. Personal areas, such as cubbies and "be by myself" spaces, are visible to teachers.			
8. An easily sanitized diapering area well stocked with supplies and a foot-operated trash can lined with a plastic bag.			
9. Child-size toilets and sinks located in a bathroom adjacent to the classroom or in a nearby hallway that children use with adult supervision.			
10. Large, open spaces containing ramps, steps, and other equipment that encourage physical activity are available indoors.			
11. Indoor spaces large enough for two or three children to play side by side.			
12. Outdoor area has designated spaces for active play by individuals or small groups of children, for construction, for gardening, for observing animals, for doing art, and for playing with sand and water.			

From *High-Quality Early Childhood Programs: The What, Why, and How* by Laura J. Colker and Derry Koralek, © 2018. Published by Redleaf Press, www.redleafpress.org. This page may be reproduced for individual or classroom use only.

2. Toddler Toys, Materials, and Equipment Observation Checklist

Toys, materials, and equipment characteristic	Observed		
	Yes	Somewhat	Not yet
1. Some of toddlers' personal items, homelike items like cushions, a tablecloth, plants, culturally significant props and play materials, and books, print, music, and other items in children's home languages are included.			
2. Books featuring families, everyday experiences, animals, and simple concepts like color and shape, numbers, and the alphabet.			
3. Blocks (soft, cardboard, and wooden), props, and accessories are available.			
4. Materials toddlers use to pretend and take on roles are available for play.			
5. Materials for filling and dumping from containers.			
6. Art materials that allow children to draw, paint, mold, print, and make collages.			
7. Rhythm instruments (both purchased and homemade), musical toys and balls, and devices such as CD players, MP3 players, or tablets are available for listening to and making music.			
8. Materials that encourage problem solving and other cognitive skills, such as pegboards, puzzles, dominoes, and lacing beads.			
9. Wheeled toys to ride, push, and pull and equipment for gross-motor activities.			
10. Natural materials that children can explore and manipulate.			
11. Unbreakable dishes, flatware, utensils, bowls, and kitchen gadgets for snack and mealtime use.			
12. Outdoor equipment and materials that promote gross-motor activity and interaction with nature.			

From *High-Quality Early Childhood Programs: The What, Why, and How* by Laura J. Colker and Derry Koralek, © 2018. Published by Redleaf Press, www.redleafpress.org. This page may be reproduced for individual or classroom use only.

3. Toddler Program Structure Checklist

Program structure characteristic	Observed		
	Yes	Somewhat	Not yet
1. A picture/photograph schedule illustrating the sequence of the day's activities hangs at toddlers' eye level.			
2. Time slots for daily activities match children's developmental capabilities.			
3. Active and quiet times are alternated throughout the day.			
4. Children play outdoors at least once a day for at least an hour.			
5. Children spend at least an hour doing activities of their own choosing, interacting with children and teachers.			
6. Teachers wait patiently as toddlers participate in routines and transitions.			
7. Teachers lead children in small-group activities.			
8. Toddlers regularly nap after lunch and get out their own blankets and lovies from home.			
9. Children sleep for as long as they need at naptime.			
10. Teachers announce to children when a transition is about to take place.			
11. Teachers are flexible about the schedule.			
12. Teachers occasionally lead unplanned activities.			

From *High-Quality Early Childhood Programs: The What, Why, and How* by Laura J. Colker and Derry Koralek, © 2018. Published by Redleaf Press, www.redleafpress.org. This page may be reproduced for individual or classroom use only.

4. Toddler Curriculum Observation Checklist

Curriculum characteristic	Observed		
	Yes	Somewhat	Not yet
1. Teachers introduce and reinforce skills based on what they observe children doing and learning.			
2. Teachers use routines and transitions as opportunities to facilitate learning.			
3. Children work independently on tasks or activities they have selected for themselves.			
4. Children play alongside others, often using the same kinds of toys.			
5. Teachers regularly observe children's interactions and activities, document what they see and hear, and maintain individual portfolios.			
6. Children use their large muscles in various activities throughout the day.			
7. Children use the small muscles in their hands in various activities throughout the day.			
8. Children engage in conversations, use language, and see print in English and their home language throughout the day.			
9. Children solve problems, explore cause and effect, and apply old knowledge to new situations throughout the day.			
10. Children express their ideas and feelings through the creative arts daily.			
11. Teachers ensure that the curriculum is accessible to all children, including those with special needs.			
12. Family members share their skills and interests and play with, read to, and otherwise engage the children.			

From *High-Quality Early Childhood Programs: The What, Why, and How* by Laura J. Colker and Derry Koralek, © 2018. Published by Redleaf Press, www.redleafpress.org. This page may be reproduced for individual or classroom use only.

5. Toddler Supportive Interactions Observation Checklist

Supportive interaction characteristic	Observed		
	Yes	Somewhat	Not yet
1. Teachers play with one or a few toddlers, modeling how to share, take turns, and use other social skills.			
2. Teachers accommodate toddlers' desires to be independent yet remain close to familiar people and places.			
3. Teachers listen to, repeat, interpret, and respond to toddlers' communications.			
4. Toddlers show empathy and concern for their peers and ask an adult for help if needed.			
5. Teachers and toddlers work together to clean up spills and messes.			
6. Teachers and toddlers hold conversations about topics of interest to the children; teachers model how to keep a conversation going.			
7. Teachers help families and toddlers reunite at the end of the day.			
8. Teachers learn and use a few important words and phrases in the toddlers' home languages.			
9. Teachers spend one-on-one time with every child at some time each day.			
10. Teachers encourage toddlers' development of new skills by responding to requests and cues as to whether teacher support is desired.			
11. Teachers use caring language, tone of voice, and physical touch to let toddlers know they are appreciated and valued.			
12. Teachers congratulate toddlers on progress and achievement of goals while watching for cues that children are ready to pursue new goals.			

From *High-Quality Early Childhood Programs: The What, Why, and How* by Laura J. Colker and Derry Koralek, © 2018. Published by Redleaf Press, www.redleafpress.org. This page may be reproduced for individual or classroom use only.

6. Toddler Positive Guidance Observation Checklist

Positive guidance characteristic	Observed		
	Yes	Somewhat	Not yet
1. The environment supports toddlers' active play and explorations while ensuring adults are comfortable.			
2. Teachers use positive statements to tell children what to do rather than what not to do.			
3. Teachers involve the toddlers in setting a few simple rules, phrased in positive terms.			
4. Teachers privately congratulate toddlers when they remember to follow the rules.			
5. Teachers review with toddlers the procedures for a neighborhood walk, field trip, or other new experience.			
6. Teachers gently hold and acknowledge the feelings of an out-of-control child during a tantrum; they help calm the child before making any suggestions.			
7. Teachers offer acceptable alternatives to address toddlers' needs or respond to their requests.			
8. Teachers read books and tell stories about typical events and challenges, using toys to help toddlers recognize, name, and manage feelings.			
9. Teachers give children time to resolve their differences; if the disagreement lasts too long, they step in to offer help.			
10. Teachers invite toddlers to say no by asking silly questions, singing songs, performing fingerplays, and reading books.			
11. Teachers provide tools, materials, time, and encouragement so toddlers can experience success.			
12. Teachers have appropriate expectations for toddlers; they give instructions for tasks.			

From *High-Quality Early Childhood Programs: The What, Why, and How* by Laura J. Colker and Derry Koralek, © 2018. Published by Redleaf Press, www.redleafpress.org. This page may be reproduced for individual or classroom use only.

Appendix D

Observation Checklists for Ensuring Quality in Preschool Programs

As you complete these checklists, you may wish to take notes regarding the status of the characteristics you observe. Add the dates of your observations if that information will be helpful to you.

1. Environment Observation Checklist

Environmental characteristic	Observed		
	Yes	Somewhat	Not yet
1. A family bulletin board / message center with current news about the program, photos of the children's activities, and samples of children's creations.			
2. Photographs of the children are prominently displayed in their cubbies and throughout the classroom.			
3. Centers are clearly defined with furnishings, flooring textures, tape, and exits to manage traffic flow.			
4. Noisy centers are separated from quiet ones.			
5. Messy activities like cooking, art, and sand/water play take place on washable flooring, while blocks, dramatic play, science, music, math and manipulatives, and literacy take place on carpeted floors.			
6. Quiet "be by myself" spaces are available where children can work/play alone or with a friend.			
7. Spaces are available to accommodate several children playing together.			
8. Materials are displayed on low shelving labeled with pictures and words in both English and the children's home languages.			
9. Print appears in English and in all the home languages of the children. When multiple home languages are present, signage is color coded to signify particular home languages.			
10. Children's art, creations, and writing samples are prominently displayed at the children's eye level.			
11. Materials and displays represent the children's cultures and family structures.			
12. Landscape features are used in the layout of the outdoor space.			

From *High-Quality Early Childhood Programs: The What, Why, and How* by Laura J. Colker and Derry Koralek, © 2018. Published by Redleaf Press, www.redleafpress.org. This page may be reproduced for individual or classroom use only.

2. Preschool Toys, Materials, and Equipment Observation Checklist

Toys, materials, and equipment characteristic	Observed		
	Yes	Somewhat	Not yet
1. Learning centers include toys and other items that respond to and build on children's interests.			
2. Every learning center includes toys, materials, and equipment that support a wide range of developmental levels. Children use some toys, materials, and equipment that are familiar and some that offer slightly greater challenges than each child's skill level.			
3. There are sufficient toys and other materials available in each learning center to support the maximum number of children allowed to play there.			
4. The toys, materials, and equipment displayed in each learning center represent only a part of the available inventory for that center.			
5. Toys, materials, and equipment are rotated periodically as children grow tired of them, develop new interests, and gain new skills.			
6. Toys and materials that are used together are displayed and stored together.			
7. Teachers add new toys, materials, and equipment to support the curriculum.			
8. There are many open-ended play items children can use in a variety of ways.			
9. Homemade and natural items supplement the purchased inventory.			
10. Children use "real" tools and safety gear under close supervision.			
11. Teachers and children bring indoor toys and materials outside regularly.			
12. Books and writing materials are found in all learning centers—not just the literacy center.			

From *High-Quality Early Childhood Programs: The What, Why, and How* by Laura J. Colker and Derry Koralek, © 2018. Published by Redleaf Press, www.redleafpress.org. This page may be reproduced for individual or classroom use only.

3. Preschool Program Structure Observation Checklist

Program structure characteristic	Observed		
	Yes	Somewhat	Not yet
1. Time slots for daily activities match children's developmental capabilities.			
2. Active and quiet times are alternated throughout the day.			
3. Children play outdoors at least once a day for at least an hour.			
4. Children spend at least an hour engaged in activities of their own choosing, including working on projects and interacting with teachers.			
5. Cleanup is ongoing, rather than being a separate item on the daily schedule.			
6. Children eat morning and afternoon snacks when they are hungry; snacks are part of child choice time rather than a separate item on the daily schedule.			
7. Children transition in small groups from being outdoors to getting ready to eat lunch.			
8. During mealtimes, adults and children pass bowls of food around the table and serve themselves family-style.			
9. Teachers and visiting family members eat a relaxed, nutritious lunch with small groups of children, engaging them in conversation.			
10. Children seamlessly transition from lunch to rest time as they finish eating.			
11. At rest time, children sleep according to their own time clocks for as long as is needed.			
12. Teachers give sufficient warning to children when a transition is about to take place.			

From *High-Quality Early Childhood Programs: The What, Why, and How* by Laura J. Colker and Derry Koralek, © 2018. Published by Redleaf Press, www.redleafpress.org. This page may be reproduced for individual or classroom use only.

4. Preschool Curriculum Observation Checklist

Curriculum characteristic	Observed		
	Yes	Somewhat	Not yet
1. Children work independently on self-selected tasks and activities. Teachers ask open-ended questions and make comments and suggestions as appropriate.			
2. Children work in pairs or small groups on cooperative activities of their choosing. Teachers pose questions and make suggestions as needed.			
3. Children do project-related work. Teachers pose inspirational questions and document children's work with photos and notes.			
4. Teachers regularly observe children's interactions and activities, document what they see and hear, and maintain individual portfolios.			
5. Teachers model prosocial behaviors and support children's use of positive behaviors, such as sharing, friendship, and empathy.			
6. Children use their large muscles in various activities throughout the day.			
7. Children use the small muscles in their hands in various activities throughout the day.			
8. Children take part in conversations and view print and its uses in English and in their home language.			
9. Children solve problems, explore cause and effect, and apply old knowledge to new situations.			
10. Children express ideas and feelings through the creative arts.			
11. Teachers ensure that the curriculum is accessible to all children, including those with special needs.			
12. Family members share their skills and interests and play with, read to, and otherwise engage the children.			

From *High-Quality Early Childhood Programs: The What, Why, and How* by Laura J. Colker and Derry Koralek, © 2018. Published by Redleaf Press, www.redleafpress.org. This page may be reproduced for individual or classroom use only.

5. Preschool Supportive Interactions Observation Checklist

Supportive interaction characteristic	Observed		
	Yes	Somewhat	Not yet
1. Teachers engage with children one-on-one, in small groups, and as the entire class.			
2. Teachers respond quickly and positively to children's needs and questions, give comfort, and help them resolve problems.			
3. Teachers bend, kneel, or sit down to establish eye contact when talking with children.			
4. Teachers attend to children who are less verbal as well as to those who have a lot to say and seek attention.			
5. Teachers show respect for children's feelings and ideas, even if they disagree with them.			
6. Teachers plan activities that encourage children to cooperate, work together, help each other, and care for one another.			
7. Teachers and children listen to other points of view and accept individual differences.			
8. Teachers encourage and offer suggestions so children can solve problems on their own, make progress, complete challenges, and learn from mistakes.			
9. Teachers help children make friends and support their efforts to renegotiate friendships as necessary.			
10. Teachers and children play, smile, laugh, and have fun while learning together.			
11. Teachers support each other during the day through gestures, facial expressions, and words.			
12. Teachers and families give each other warm greetings and updates about children's experiences and progress.			

From *High-Quality Early Childhood Programs: The What, Why, and How* by Laura J. Colker and Derry Koralek, © 2018. Published by Redleaf Press, www.redleafpress.org. This page may be reproduced for individual or classroom use only.

6. Preschool Positive Guidance Observation Checklist

Positive guidance characteristic	Observed		
	Yes	Somewhat	Not yet
1. The environment is safe, well planned, and developmentally appropriate.			
2. Teachers involve children in setting a few important, positively stated rules.			
3. Teachers acknowledge children's strong feelings, while guiding them to express those feelings through words or cope with them through another outlet.			
4. Teachers describe desired actions in positive terms that tell children what is expected.			
5. Teachers introduce a simple conflict resolution process and remind children to use it when disagreements arise.			
6. Teachers provide many opportunities for preschoolers to make choices throughout the day.			
7. Teachers include children in doing valued tasks that keep the environment safe and tidy.			
8. Teachers stop or adjust what they are doing to address the needs of a child who is distressed.			
9. Once a child is no longer acting out and has regained self-control, teachers have a private discussion with the child.			
10. Teachers consider the reasons underlying a child's behavior.			
11. Teachers involve families in helping a child replace challenging behaviors with appropriate ones.			
12. Teachers help children who use bullying behaviors as well as children who are bullied.			

From *High-Quality Early Childhood Programs: The What, Why, and How* by Laura J. Colker and Derry Koralek, © 2018. Published by Redleaf Press, www.redleafpress.org. This page may be reproduced for individual or classroom use only.

Appendix E

Observation Checklist for Engaging Families in Early Childhood Programs

As you complete this checklist, you may wish to take notes regarding the status of the strategies used to engage families. Add the date you completed the checklist if that information will be helpful to you.

Observation Checklist

ENGAGING FAMILIES IN EARLY CHILDHOOD PROGRAMS

Family engagement strategy	Observed		
	Yes	*Somewhat*	*Not yet*
1. Teachers provide an orientation to the program for children and families at the start of the year and as needed when new families enroll.			
2. Teachers greet family members by name at pickup and drop-off times; teachers correctly pronounce everyone's name.			
3. Teachers and families exchange information about the child regularly.			
4. Teachers provide news and updates about the children's activities on a regular schedule and through multiple venues in all languages used by families.			
5. Families have a designated resource area and a comfortable area for nursing mothers and bottle-feeding in the infant room.			
6. Teachers encourage family members to participate in the program by sharing a skill, interest, or aspect of their home language and culture.			
7. Teachers, staff, and families plan events on topics of interest to families.			
8. Teachers and families have regular conferences to share information, review the child's progress, and plan ways to support the child at home and at the program in the future.			
9. Teachers and families plan and participate in program-wide events, involving children, parents, and staff in enjoyable activities.			
10. Older toddlers and preschoolers eagerly show their families photos and examples of their work and learning displayed in the classroom.			
11. Teachers provide an orientation and resources for family members who are classroom volunteers; they ask family members what they would be comfortable doing with the children.			
12. Teachers welcome family members to visit the classroom at any time during the day; family members do not need to have an appointment to drop in.			

From *High-Quality Early Childhood Programs: The What, Why, and How* by Laura J. Colker and Derry Koralek, © 2018. Published by Redleaf Press, www.redleafpress.org. This page may be reproduced for individual or classroom use only.

Appendix F

Resources for Supporting Quality in Early Childhood Programs

Organizations

For further information on providing high-quality care for infants, toddlers, and preschoolers, please consult one or more of the organizations listed here:

Association for Childhood Education International (ACEI)
1200 18th Street NW, Suite 700
Washington, DC 20036
(202) 372-9986 or (800) 423-3563

www.acei.org

Child Care Aware of America (formerly the National Association of Child Care Resource and Referral Agencies [NACCRRA])
1515 N. Courthouse Road, 3rd Floor
Arlington, VA 22201
(703) 341-4100 or (800) 424-2246

http://usa.childcareaware.org

Division for Early Childhood (DEC) of the Council for Exceptional Children
2900 Crystal Drive, Suite 100
Arlington, VA 22202
(310) 428-7209
www.dec-sped.org

Military Child Education Coalition (MCEC)
909 Mountain Lion Circle
Harker Heights, TX 76548
(254) 953-1923

www.militarychild.org

National Association for the Education of Young Children (NAEYC)
1313 L Street NW, Suite 500
Washington, DC 20005
(202) 232-8777 or (800) 424-2460

www.naeyc.org

National Black Child Development Institute (NBCDI)
8455 Colesville Road, Suite 820
Silver Spring, MD 20910
(202) 833-2220 or (800) 556-2234

www.nbcdi.org

National Head Start Association (NHSA)
1651 Prince Street
Alexandria, VA 22314
(703) 739-0875 or (866) 677-8724

www.nhsa.org

Society for Research in Child Development (SRCD)
1825 K Street NW, Suite 325
Washington, DC 20006
(202) 800-0677

www.srcd.org

Southern Early Childhood Association (SECA)
1123 S. University Avenue, Suite 255
Little Rock, AR 72204
(501) 221-1648 or (800) 305-7322

www.southernearlychildhood.org

WestEd
730 Harrison Street
San Francisco, CA 94107
(415) 565-3000 or (877) 493-7833

www.wested.org

Zero to Three: National Center for Infants, Toddlers and Families
1255 23rd Street NW, Suite 350
Washington, DC 20037
(202) 638-1144

www.zerotothree.org

Journals

The following journals provide research and information on best practices in early childhood education:

Child Development
SRCD
1825 K Street NW, Suite 325
Washington, DC 20006
(202) 800-0677
www.srcd.org/publications
/child-development

Early Childhood Research Quarterly
Elsevier
230 Park Avenue, Suite 800
New York, NY 10169
(202) 232-8777 or (800) 424-2460
www.journals.elsevier.com
/early-childhood-research-quarterly

Educational Researcher
American Educational Research Association
(AERA)
1430 K Street NW, Suite 1200
Washington, DC 20005
(202) 238-3200
www.aera.net/Publications

Exchange
Child Care Information Exchange
17725 NE 65th Street, B-275
Redmond, WA 98052
(425) 883-9394 or (800) 221-2864
www.childcareexchange.com

International Journal of Early Childhood Special Education (INTJECSE)
Professor Dr. Ibrahim H. Diken
Anadolu University, Research Institute for Individuals with Disabilities
Anadolu University Yunus Emre Campus 26470
Eskisehir, Turkey
+90-222-335-2914
www.int-jecse.net

Teaching Young Children (TYC)
NAEYC
1313 L Street NW, Suite 500
Washington, DC 20005
(202) 232-8777 or (800) 424-2460
www.naeyc.org/tyc

Young Children (YC)
NAEYC
1313 L Street NW, Suite 500
Washington, DC 20005
(202) 232-8777 or (800) 424-2460
www.naeyc.org/yc

Books

There are many books that you may wish to consult to learn more about high-quality early childhood education programs. Here are some suggested titles:

Bloom, Paula Jorde, Ann Hentschel, and Jill Bella. 2013. *Inspiring Peak Performance: Competence, Commitment, and Collaboration.* St. Paul, MN: Redleaf Press.

Bruno, Holly Elissa. 2011. *What You Need to Lead an Early Childhood Program: Emotional Intelligence in Practice.* Washington, DC: NAEYC.

Campbell-Barr, Verity, and Caroline Leeson. 2016. *Quality and Leadership in the Early Years: Research, Theory, and Practice.* Thousand Oaks, CA: Sage Publications.

Copple, Carol, and Sue Bredekamp, eds. 2009. *Developmentally Appropriate Practice in Early Childhood Programs Serving Children from Birth through Age 8.* 3rd ed. Washington, DC: NAEYC.

Curtis, Deb, and Margie Carter. 2012. *The Art of Awareness: How Observation Can Transform Your Teaching.* 2nd ed. St. Paul, MN: Redleaf Press.

Curtis, Deb, and Margie Carter. 2009. *The Visionary Director: A Handbook for Dreaming, Organizing, and Improvising in Your Center.* 2nd ed. St. Paul, MN: Redleaf Press.

Dahlburg, Gunilla, Peter Moss, and Alan Pence. 2013. *Beyond Quality in Early Childhood Education and Care: Languages of Evaluation.* 3rd ed. London: Routledge Publications.

Derman-Sparks, Louise, Debbie Lee Keenan, and John Nimmo. 2015. *Leading Anti-Bias Early Childhood Programs: A Guide for Change.* New York: Teachers College Press.

Dombro, Amy Laura, Judy Jablon, and Charlotte Stetson. 2011. *Powerful Interactions: How to Connect with Children to Extend Their Learning.* Washington, DC: NAEYC.

Epstein, Ann S. 2015. *The Intentional Teacher: Choosing the Best Strategies for Young Children's Learning.* Washington, DC: NAEYC.

Gonzalez-Mena, Janet. 2013. *50 Strategies for Communicating and Working with Diverse Families.* 3rd ed. Boston: Pearson.

Harris Helm, Judy, and Lilian G. Katz. 2016. *Young Investigators: The Project Approach in the Early Years.* 3rd ed. New York: Teachers College Press.

Hyson, Marilou. 2008. *Enthusiastic and Engaged Learners: Approaches to Learning in the Early Childhood Classroom.* New York: Teachers College Press.

Isbell, Rebecca, and Sonia Akiko Yoshizawa. 2017. *Nurturing Creativity: An Essential Mindset for Young Children's Learning.* Washington, DC: NAEYC.

Jablon, Judy, Amy Laura Dombro, and Shaun Johnsen. 2016. *Coaching with Powerful Interactions: A Guide for Partnering with Early Childhood Teachers.* Washington, DC: NAEYC.

Lally, J. Ronald. 2008. *Caring for Infants and Toddlers in Groups: Developmentally Appropriate Practice.* 2nd ed. Washington, DC: Zero to Three.

Nemeth, Karen N. 2009. *Many Languages, One Classroom: Teaching Dual and English Language Learners*. Lewisville, NC: Gryphon House.

Nemeth, Karen N. 2012. *Many Languages, Building Connections: Supporting Infants and Toddlers Who Are Dual Language Learners*. Lewisville, NC: Gryphon House.

OECD (Organisation for Economic Co-operation and Development). 2015. *Starting Strong IV: Monitoring Quality in Early Childhood Education and Care: Edition 2015*. Paris: OECD Publishing.

Penn, Helen. 2011. *Quality in Early Childhood Services: An International Perspective*. Maidenhead, UK: Open University Press.

Schweikert, Gigi. 2013. *Being a Supervisor: Winning Ways for Early Childhood Professionals*. St. Paul, MN: Redleaf Press.

Singer, Dorothy, Roberta Michnick Golinkoff, and Kathy Hirsh-Pasek. 2009. *Play = Learning: How Play Motivates and Enhances Children's Cognitive and Social-Emotional Growth*. Oxford, UK: Oxford University Press.

Slaughter, Emma. 2016. *Quality in the Early Years*. Maidenhead, UK: Open University Press.

Souto-Manning, Mariana. 2013. *Multicultural Teaching in the Early Childhood Classroom: Approaches, Strategies, and Tools, Preschool–2nd Grade*. New York: Teachers College Press.

Sullivan, Debra Ren-Etta. 2009. *Learning to Lead: Effective Leadership Skills for Teachers of Young Children*. 2nd ed. St. Paul, MN: Redleaf Press.

References

Adamson-Kain, Stephanie. 2014. "Memo to: Preschool Teachers Everywhere: Children Need and Have a Right to Play." *Young Children* 69 (2): 16.

Administration for Children and Families, US Department of Health and Human Services. 2015. *Caring for Our Children Basics: Health and Safety Foundations for Early Care and Education.* Washington, DC. www.acf.hhs.gov/sites/default/files/ecd/caring_for_our_children _basics.pdf.

American Academy of Pediatrics, American Public Health Association, and National Resource Center for Health and Safety in Child Care and Early Education. 2011. *Caring for Our Children: National Health and Safety Performance Standards; Guidelines for Early Care and Education Programs.* 3rd ed. Elk Grove Village, IL: American Academy of Pediatrics.

Center on the Developing Child at Harvard University. 2007. *The Science of Early Childhood Development* (InBrief). http://developingchild.harvard.edu/resources/inbrief-science-of-ecd.

Click, Phyllis M., Kimberly A. Karkos, and Cathie Robertson. 2013. *Administration of Programs for Young Children.* 9th ed. Stamford, CT: Cengage.

Colker, Laura J. 2008. "Twelve Characteristics of Effective Early Childhood Teachers." *Young Children* on the Web. March. www.naeyc.org/files/yc/file/200803/BTJ_Colker.pdf.

———. 2009. *Sure Start Program Guide.* Alexandria, VA: Department of Defense Education Activity.

Dodge, Diane Trister, Cate Heroman, Laura J. Colker, Toni S. Bickart, Kai-leé Berke, and Heather Baker. 2016. *The Creative Curriculum for Preschool.* Vol. 1, The Foundation. 6th ed. Bethesda, MD: Teaching Strategies.

Dodge, Diane Trister, Sherrie Rudick, and Kai-leé Berke. 2011. *The Creative Curriculum for Infants, Toddlers, and Twos.* Vol. 2, Routines and Experiences. Bethesda, MD: Teaching Strategies.

Gillespie, Linda Groves, and Nancy L. Seibel. 2006. "Self-Regulation: A Cornerstone of Early Childhood Development." *Young Children* on the Web. www.naeyc.org/files/yc/file /200607/Gillespie709BTJ.pdf.

Halgunseth, Linda, Amy Peterson, Deborah R. Stark, and Shannon Moodie. 2009. *Family Engagement, Diverse Families, and Early Childhood Education Programs: An Integrated Review of the Literature.* Washington, DC: NAEYC. www.naeyc.org/files/naeyc/file/research /FamEngage.pdf.

Jablon, Judy, Amy Laura Dombro, and Shaun Johnsen. 2014. *Coaching with Powerful Interactions: A Guide for Partnering with Early Childhood Teachers.* Washington, DC: NAEYC.

NAEYC and NACCRRA. 2011. *Early Childhood Education Professional Development: Training and Technical Assistance Glossary.* Washington, DC: NAEYC. www.naeyc.org/Glossary Training_TA.pdf.

NAEYC.2009. NAEYC Standards for Early Childhood Professional Preparation Programs. Washington, DC: NAEYC. www.naeyc.org/file/positions/ProfPrepStandards09.pdf.

———. 2011. *Code of Ethical Conduct and Statement of Commitment.* Washington, DC: NAEYC. www.naeyc.org/files/naeyc/image/public_policy/Ethics%20Position%20Statement2011 _09202013update.pdf.

———. 2017. "Principles of Effective Practice: Family Engagement." Accessed June 13. www .naeyc.org/familyengagement/principles.

Office of Head Start. 2017. "Head Start Policy and Regulations." https://eclkc.ohs.acf.hhs.gov /policy/45-cfr-chap-xiii/1302-21-center-based-option.

Shonkoff, Jack P., and Deborah A. Phillips, eds. 2000. *From Neurons to Neighborhoods: The Science of Early Childhood Development.* Washington, DC: National Academy Press.

US Consumer Product Safety Commission. 2012. *Toy Safety.* www.cpsc.gov/Business-- Manufacturing/Business-Education/Toy-Safety#T1.

US Department of Education, 2011. "Definitions." www.ed.gov/early-learning/elc-draft -summary/definitions.

Washington, Valora, ed. 2017. *Essentials for Working with Young Children.* 2nd ed. Washington, DC: Council for Professional Recognition.

Index

as foundation for learning, 44

primary caregiver and, 39

responding to children's needs promptly
and consistently and, 23, 36, 44,
52, 129

supportive interactions and, 46

using home language and, 48

University of Northern Iowa, 13

US Department of Education

definition of domains of school
readiness, 6

definition of early learning and
developmental standards, 6

Vygotsky, Lev, 122

young infants

art activities for, 45

defined, 119